You'll Never Walk Alone

D0367500

Publications International, Ltd.

Christine A. Dallman (contributing writer) is the author of *Daily Devotions for Seniors*, an inspirational resource for maturing adults. She is also the coauthor of several other titles including *How to Let God Help You Through Hard Times* and *If Jesus Loves Me, How Do I Know?*

Additional stories contributed by:
Stacy Lee Athens, "A Special Shopping Trip" (pp. 147–150); **Glenda Barrett,** "Bracing Up" (pp. 33–37); **Margaret Cheasebro,** "A Gift of Love" (pp. 82–88); **Jackie Clements-Marenda,** "The Dance" (pp. 8–13); **Christine A. Dallman** (as told by Loyal Dallman-Arnold), "A Gift of Time" (pp. 169–170); **Karen M. Leet,** "Diapers" (pp. 51–54); **Lena J. Moser,** "Even a Snickers Bar" (pp. 45–48); **Deby Murray,** "When Angels Kiss" (pp. 58–63); **Diane Nichols** (as told by Josh Wright), "My Father's Love" (pp. 179–186); **Luis Perez, Jr.,** "Just Friends" (pp. 133–138); **Michele J. Rader,** "The Scenic Route" (pp. 69–74); **Frances E. Sames** (as told by Robbie Morris), "Guiding Lights" (pp. 121–124); **Kristina M. Santos,** "Front-Porch Petunias" (pp. 158–161); **Carol Solstad,** "Rescued on the Roadside" (pp. 21–27); **Linda Thompson-Penny,** "Christmas Cookies" (pp. 106–112); and **Betty Toole,** "Friday Nights" (pp. 93–100).

Louis Weber, CEO
Publications International, Ltd.
7373 North Cicero Avenue
Lincolnwood, Illinois 60712

Manufactured in U.S.A.

8 7 6 5 4 3 2

ISBN-13: 978-1-4127-1008-4
ISBN-10: 1-4127-1008-1

Contents

Journeying with God 5

CHAPTER 1
He Holds Those Who Mourn 7

CHAPTER 2
As Hope Ebbs, God's Goodness Flows 20

CHAPTER 3
Suffering Loss and Yet Being Found 32

CHAPTER 4
Our Neediness: A Place to Meet God 44

CHAPTER 5
He Carries Our Cares 57

CHAPTER 6
A Hero for the Helpless 68

CHAPTER 7
When We Fail, God Stands by Us 81

CHAPTER 8
A Friend to the Lonely *92*

CHAPTER 9
Abandoned but Not Forsaken *105*

CHAPTER 10
Kept Safe in Danger *120*

CHAPTER 11
When We Doubt God's Goodness *132*

CHAPTER 12
He Frees Us from Depression *146*

CHAPTER 13
A Healer for the Hurting *157*

CHAPTER 14
With Us in the Shadow of Death *168*

CHAPTER 15
He Loves the Unloved *178*

∽∾∽

Journeying with God

We often think of life in terms of a journey—a walk through time in which we experience joy and sorrow, pleasure and pain, peace and turmoil. In the course of a lifetime, as we continue along—daily, weekly, monthly, yearly—upon the unique terrain of our own lifescape, it can sometimes seem as though we are traveling alone.

The stories included in this book are personal accounts of such times in the lives of people who have walked through the barren desert of difficulty. For many, it seemed as though they would become hopelessly stranded in their personal desert with no one to come alongside them with help. Yet in each case, there was a wonderful discovery: At no time were they ever walking alone!

You may be experiencing your own trek through a desert place in life. It may feel as if the sun is scorching your mind and heart, the sand is blinding your spiritual eyes, your water supply (faith) is dangerously low, and you do not have a sense of direction or even of hope. Worst of all, you might be feeling all alone with no one to hear you call out for help. You need to know that you are not alone. God is there with you, and he will see you through your desert experience.

It's not necessary to read this book in order, front to back. If you are struggling with a particular issue or need, scan the Contents to find a chapter title that sounds relevant to you, and begin there. There are stories, prayers, Bible verses, and devotional thoughts to encourage your heart and remind you that God is always with you. He will never abandon you in your desert. So take heart today! God sees you, he cares about you, he is with you, and he will help you. With him by your side, you will never walk alone.

CHAPTER 1

He Holds Those Who Mourn

*I*n God's heart there's a special place for grief-stricken people. He looks with compassion on those who mourn and promises to comfort them. It may seem to us, though, in the most inconsolable moments of our grief, that there could not possibly be a time or a place where our souls will be soothed. It doesn't seem possible that we will find healing even in God's embrace. Even so, he remains close to us and keeps watch over us until we can be comforted by his love.

The Dance

"My dad wants you to tell your dad that he'll drive Friday night. Why take two cars when we're going to the same place?"

The words uttered by one classmate to another reach my ears despite the noisy chatter of three dozen other 13-year-olds rushing through the school hallway to their next class.

"Is your dad's car big enough for the four of us? I don't want my dress to get squished. We should..."

The second girl's voice trails off, and I know it's because they have noticed me standing by my locker. Their topic of discussion is the upcoming father-daughter dance, but I won't be attending. A father is necessary, and cancer claimed mine just a few months ago.

I pretend to be interested in my locker contents, thus giving the duo a chance to pass me by without further comment. In this small, all-girl Catholic high school, I'm the only one who has buried a parent, and nobody, including myself, is exactly sure how to deal with this. Silence seems to be the acceptable solution.

Every year the school has a father-daughter dance. It's a fund-raising event to help pay for the extra supplies the school needs. The students pick a theme, decorate the gym, and solicit raffle donations from local businesses. There are committees for everything from setup to cleanup, and all students are urged to participate.

"I know how difficult this is for you, Jacquelyn," Sister Patricia says when she catches me gazing at a poster advertising the premier school event of 1967. "But life moves forward. In time you will be able to talk about your father without tears."

I'm sure she's wrong! I cry myself to sleep every night, and I avoid the movie theater where Dad and I used to attend the cowboy marathon extravaganza every month. I worry constantly, too, but not about passing algebra and chemistry. I fear I will forget the sound of my father's voice.

"Your father is gone, and you must make a life without him," Sister Patricia says as she points to the sign-up sheets tacked to the bulletin board beside the poster. "Start by helping out with some aspect of the dance. Sell raffle tickets or serve the lemonade."

I don't want a life without him! Why is this so hard for Sister to understand? I want my dad here with me now! We had plans—many, many plans—things we would do together... things that now will never be done.

Friday night I'm in my pajamas by 6:00. If I can force myself to sleep, I won't think about the dance. Then, on Monday, maybe I'll come down with some disease that will keep me out of school until the after-event talk becomes old news.

Suddenly I hear our apartment doorbell ring, then the sound of my Uncle Edmund's voice. Edmund is my father's brother, a bachelor by choice. Usually he stops by every Sunday afternoon for a visit, but today isn't Sunday. Is something wrong? Filled with curiosity, I venture from my bedroom to investigate.

Uncle Edmund is dressed in his best black suit. At the sight of me, he smiles and remarks, "I hope you aren't planning to wear pajamas to the school dance. I believe something fancier is required."

All color drains from my face, and my throat tightens. I look to my mother for help, for her to tell Uncle Edmund I can't go to the dance with him. Yes, he's a wonderful uncle, and I love him, but this dance is for fathers and their daughters.

"I figured you'd forget to buy the tickets, so I stopped by the school and picked them up." Uncle Edmund smiles at me. "I sneaked a peek at the gym, too. It looks great with all the flowers, rainbows, and stars. What's this year's theme?"

"Feeling Groovy." My mouth is as dry as cotton. Why didn't the person who sold Uncle Edmund the tickets tell him what this dance is all about? "But I can't . . ."

"You're right," Uncle Edmund interrupts. "You can't begin to get ready until I give you the other ticket." From his front jacket pocket he takes out a small orange ticket, identical to the ones used at the movie theater. He hands it to me with the instruction, "Read what's written on the back."

I turn the ticket over, instantly recognizing my father's handwriting. On this ticket my father wrote: "Good for one father event."

"Your father fought very hard to live, but when he realized he couldn't win the battle, he turned his attention to your future," Uncle Edmund softly explains. "He filled out over a hundred such tickets and gave them to me to hold. I promised him I'd make sure you did with me all you had planned to do with him. That includes this dance. I spoke to your school principal, and she agrees with the validity of this ticket. Substitute dads are acceptable escorts."

Tears blind me. I can't move or think. Even though my dad is no longer here with me, he is still taking care of me.

Reaching out, my uncle uses a fingertip to wipe away my tears. "Hurry now. You get ready while I go pick up your corsage. Your mother says the dress you wore to Vincent's wedding is perfect for tonight." He clicks his heels together. "We don't want to miss the dance contest. I do a mean tango."

Uncle Edmund and I attend the father-daughter dance that night, and in the years that follow we use tickets stating things such as "Good for one Broadway show," "Good for one prom dress shopping spree," and "Good for one high school graduation dinner." Eventually Uncle Edmund learns to like Roy Rogers movies; I learn to tango. In time, as Sister Patricia predicted, I could even talk about my dad and smile.

I don't think any child ever gets over the death of a parent. However, I consider myself lucky that my father loved me so much he unselfishly helped his only brother become my hero. Because of Uncle Edmund, I was able to do many of the things my dad and I had planned to do. And even though Dad wasn't actually there with me, he has always been present in my heart.

Dear heavenly Father, because you made me, you know my grief as though it were your own. Please help me receive the comfort you bring to me through others, through your Word, and through the whispers of your Spirit to my heart. I need you more than ever right now. Thank you for walking with me through this sorrow. In Jesus' name. Amen.

Blessed are those who mourn, for they will be comforted.

Matthew 5:4

I sense the nearness of your presence, Lord Jesus, even in the shadowy places of grief. When the pain is so big that I cannot bear it, thank you that you hold me together, that you hold me close to your heart. Even though I can see life only through my tears right now, I can feel you carrying me along toward

days when I will be able to find happiness again. Let me be consoled by your nearness today.

Sorrow and sighing shall flee away. I, I am he who comforts you.... For I am the Lord your God.

Isaiah 51:11–12, 15

Psychologists have helped us understand that grieving is a necessary process to help us work through the pain of a great loss. When we allow ourselves to grieve, we are receiving God's own prescription for our emotional healing. Moving through the steps of our grief, however, may sometimes cause us to feel weak, vulnerable, afraid. At such times we may be tempted to close off our emotions and withdraw from the grieving process. But we can press on, for God is walking with us, and he will give us the courage and strength to get to healing.

Your faithful companionship is what is consoling me right now, O God. Sometimes my family and friends don't feel comfortable around my grief. Maybe they're afraid of saying or doing the wrong thing. I can understand that, and I know that they still care. But thank you, dear Lord, for not staying away. You wait in silence with me, and you speak truth and love to me when I need it most. My faith in you is growing as I realize how perfectly you understand and how carefully you watch over my life. Thank you for staying with me.

C. S. Lewis, author of the *Chronicles of Narnia,* married late in life, and he was not married many years before he lost his wife, Joy, to cancer. After her death, Lewis kept a journal, which was later published under the title *A Grief Observed*. In this small volume, the author's honesty—his anguish, his anger, his fear, his loneliness, his questions—is sometimes unsettling. But the truthfulness of what he admits about his struggle breaks the uncomfortable silence that often surrounds the issues of a grieving heart. And in Lewis's openness about his experience, the reader discovers that God does not reject us in our struggle with grief. God is not afraid of what we are thinking and feeling, no matter how terrible it may seem to us. Rather, he chooses to walk with us through it, helping us to heal along the way.

Let your steadfast love become my comfort according to your promise.... Let your mercy come to me, that I may live.

Psalm 119:76–77

Lord God, I experience your comforting love for me in so many ways. Cards and phone calls come from friends and family who want to tell me they are thinking of me and praying for me. You send a timely message to me in the form of a poem, an article, a sermon. And just seeing or being in your creation

holds a special healing balm for my soul. Thank you, Father. All these things tell me again and again: You are near.

It's comforting to realize that our God does not just know *about* our grief; he has tasted it firsthand. The Scriptures tell us that Jesus was a man of sorrows and familiar with grief. So his comfort is not based in mere sympathy but in true empathy. He feels our pain with us, and he has carried our sorrow and grief himself on the cross. As he walks with us in our times of mourning, we can trust that he knows precisely what we are feeling and understands how to see us through.

Then I saw a new heaven and a new earth. . . . And I heard a loud voice from the throne saying, "See, the home of God is among mortals. He will dwell with them. . . . He will wipe every tear from

their eyes. Death will be no more; mourning and crying and pain will be no more, for the first things have passed away."

Revelation 21:1, 3–4

God of my life, the darkness of my grief cannot shut out the light of your comforting love. It glows softly, warmly even as I weep, and I know that you are holding me close. Thank you for staying with me through this dark night. I know that you will carry me to a place of consolation and then, one day, to joy again. But for now, I'm satisfied just to know the soothing tenderness of your presence that causes me to know I am not walking this path alone.

CHAPTER 2

As Hope Ebbs, God's Goodness Flows

*W*e can live without many things, but we cannot live without hope. Yet, when life's circumstances deal us one discouraging blow after another, hope can get knocked right out of us. Sometimes it can feel as if we don't even have a breath left to lift a prayer. "Why bother," we tell ourselves. "It's hopeless." That is an old fatal lie that we must resist with our last ounce of strength. As long as there is a breath of life in us, there is hope. Why? Because there is a God, and he is good.

Rescued on the Roadside

Hot and bitter. Prickly and sweaty. Alienated and full of self-pity. That's how I felt. It was summer in the Deep South, and I was standing on the side of an isolated two-lane road in the middle of nowhere with the flattest-looking tire I'd ever seen. It certainly hadn't been a good day. It hadn't even been a good year.

Sitting down on the edge of the backseat, looking out at the pastoral nothingness, I felt exhausted. Only the sight of my three-year-old son, Ian, sleeping in the car seat beside me provided any relief from the feelings that were overwhelming me. God was handing me one stinking, rotten deal after another. I knew my faith was being tested, and I was flunking the test.

I had set out on the ill-fated 200-mile round-trip drive for a job interview with new tires on my freshly tuned-up car. At least we would have a safe trip with no mishaps, I thought. Wrong. The interview hadn't even gone well. So now I was on my way back home to a low-paying newspaper job—assuming I could ever get back on the road. I enjoyed my job, but I was tired of eating cereal three meals a day, of constantly worrying about money, and of feeling so unbearably alone all the time. Everything was a challenge, from finding decent child care to paying for medical insurance, from keeping my battered old car running to finding peace and contentment for even a minute. I was anxious, overextended, and desperate much of the time. It seemed that the harder I tried, the farther behind I got. I wanted a break.

I knew our situation wasn't much different from that of a lot of single-parent families. But I criticized myself for not doing well, and then I scolded myself for feeling bad about my failures. It was a downward emotional spiral.

Even the bit of good luck I recently had took a sour turn. When I found out about the interview, it turned out that a friend's family lived in the same town. They offered to take care of Ian while I went to the interview. But when I drove back to the pretty little farm to pick up Ian, he seemed happier than ever surrounded by a large and loving family—a family that I couldn't give him. I drove away feeling depressed and angry. I couldn't even be glad that Ian had enjoyed such a nice day.

I took a swig of water from the thermos I had prudently brought along. Then, after checking on my son, I took the spare out of the trunk, along with the tire iron and the jack. I got the car jacked up and then went to work on the lug nuts. My geriatric car had long since lost its hubcaps. I tried to turn the last rusty nut, but it wouldn't budge. I was getting sweatier and more aggravated. My hand slipped, and I scraped the middle knuckle of my right hand. Blood gushed everywhere. I grabbed some tissues and applied direct pressure, trying to remember when I'd had my last tetanus shot. I sat down next to Ian and gave in to my tears. Through my sobs, I asked God what I had done wrong. It wasn't just the tire, the heat, and the bad interview—it was my whole pathetic life and, even worse, the life I was giving my son.

Cars zipped by, and no one stopped. I just sat and cried. I felt totally helpless. I was so overwhelmed that

I didn't even hear the people approach. I was startled when I heard a woman's soft voice asking, "Are you all right?"

I was embarrassed to be caught crying. "My tire's flat, and I can't get the lug nut off."

"What did you do to your hand?" asked a male voice. I looked up into a face so scarred it was hard to look at him.

"The tire," I said, pointing to the culprit.

"You got water?" he asked.

I told him I did. He reached for the thermos and poured the cold water over my hand, then gently wiped it with the tissue. Reaching into his wallet, he pulled out an adhesive bandage and placed it on my knuckle. Not a single word passed between us the whole time.

The young woman looked at Ian, who was sleeping soundly. "He's a cutie," she said, smiling. She was pretty, with an open, vivacious face. "Waldo will fix your tire. He's good at mechanical things."

Waldo was already loosening the lug nut. If I hadn't been so hot and tired, I would have felt a little humiliated, but I was too close to heat prostration to care. My son stirred. As soon as he opened his eyes and spotted the smiling woman, he started grinning.

"Your spare's real bad. You need to get a new one," Waldo said.

"Great," I muttered, "another problem."

The woman identified herself as Laurie. She played patty-cake and peekaboo with a delighted Ian while Waldo finished his labors.

"You're all set," Waldo said, a beautiful smile brightening and softening his ravaged face.

"We've gotta go," Laurie said, waving good-bye to Ian. "It's almost time for supper, and then we've got church."

"About a mile down the road," Waldo told me, "there's a service station. My friend Billy works there, and he'll fix you up with a good tire cheap. You gotta replace the tire I put on. It's really bad. Then you need to get a new spare, too. I'll call him from the house to let him know you're coming. You take care."

Waldo and Laurie ran off down the embankment toward a dilapidated mobile home park. Both of them turned and waved. I waved back.

When I got to the service station, Billy was waiting. He handed me a soda. "Waldo said to fix you up with a good used tire 'cause your spare's shot. I got one here I'll let you have for eight bucks. I won't charge you no labor on account of Waldo sending you." While he worked, he talked—Billy was a talker. He told me he had grown up with Waldo. They'd gone to Vietnam together. "He got hurt over there," Billy said. He took his greasy hands and made a circle motion over his face. "When he came back, he had to go through a lot of surgeries for his injuries. He was engaged to Laurie's sister, and she dumped him."

"And Laurie...?" I asked.

"Well," he smiled, "we all used to kid him before the war about Laurie having a crush on him. He always laughed if off 'cause he'd been going with her sister since junior high. But when he came back, it was Laurie that was there for him. She'd visit him in the hospital. She'd read to him and sing songs for him. Then, when he got out, she'd drive him to his rehabilitation visits. Bit by bit, we all saw it coming—he just fell for that girl. They're planning to get married soon." He stood up. "You're good to go."

I thanked Billy. He said he always takes care of anyone Waldo sends his way. I wondered how many people Waldo and Laurie have rescued. A man who carries bandages, and a girl with a healing smile.

That was 20 years ago. And two decades later, I still remember those good Samaritans and their faces and voices as if it were yesterday. They fixed a lot more than a flat tire that day. They gave a broken-hearted young mother renewed faith in humanity and in herself. They gave her hope to carry on.

Lord, I am often tempted to look for hope in circumstances and opportunities that come up or that I can manufacture. Help me lay down my hope in these things. I want to put my

hope in you so that whether circumstances work out the way I want them to or not, I am trusting that you are orchestrating the events in my life for a wonderful purpose.

May the God of hope fill you with all joy and peace in believing, so that you may abound in hope by the power of the Holy Spirit.

Romans 15:13

Sometimes it hurts to hope again. We have hoped and been disappointed. But perhaps there is something we have missed about hope along the way. Perhaps we have misunderstood what it means to have hope. We often put our hope in specific things. This is not true hope, however. True hope looks to God, not people or circumstances, to give us everything we need. True hope admits that we do not know the future and, therefore, we need God to show us the path of life.

True hope does not count on the behavior of other people to determine how it will react. True hope knows in its heart of hearts that God exists and that he is good. It does not seek to determine outcomes; it simply knows that God loves us and will never fail us and looks expectantly to him for all things.

Now faith is the assurance of things hoped for, the conviction of things not seen.

Hebrews 11:1

Father, I admit that I have given up hope sometimes because I have misplaced my hopes and have made demands on you and others that I have no right to make. Please heal my disappointment and fear. Teach me how to place my hope in you the way the Bible reveals I can. I'm looking forward to learning how to walk this new path with you.

There is a great scene in *Homeward Bound*, a movie about the misadventures of two dogs and a cat who travel through the wilderness to be reunited with their owners. At the very end of the film, the cat and the younger dog have made it back to the children to whom they belong. But the older dog, Shadow, is nowhere to be seen. Peter, Shadow's boy, eagerly searches the horizon and calls his dog's name. Finally, he turns back toward his parents, close to tears, and says, "He was too old.... He was just too old."

But just when all hope had ebbed away, the old golden retriever comes limping over the hill, tired and weak, but determined to be with his boy. The joy of the reunion is deeply moving, the highlight of the movie.

God is determined to be with us no matter what. Although he is not old nor decrepit and his ability to save us is not in question, still sometimes it seems to us as if he will not show up. Nothing could be farther from the truth. Hang on to your hope in God; you will never be disappointed.

We boast in our hope of sharing the glory of God.... and hope does not disappoint us, because God's love has been poured into our hearts through the Holy Spirit that has been given to us.

Romans 5:2, 5

My Father, grant me renewed hope in you alone. Forgive me for misplacing my hope in things that are not you. I know you are faithful, that you never fail, and that you are worthy of my devotion. When my hope ebbs away, let your goodness flow into my life to help me remain steadfast. Thank you that you are here walking with me in my circumstances. I look past everything that is threatening to trouble me right now and will abide in true hope. You are my hope. Amen.

CHAPTER 3

Suffering Loss and Yet Being Found

*O*ne of the great men of faith in the Bible is Job, who lost his children and his wealth. Moreover, his health took such a turn for the worse that his wife encouraged him to just give up and die. Yet, Job remained faithful to the Lord. His secret had everything to do with his relationship with God. Job was confident—confident even while he grieved—that however great and painful his losses in this life, he would never become lost in despair as long as his God was walking with him.

Bracing Up

Unable to hold back the tears, I buried my head in my pillow and cried. I hoped no one would notice, but the kind physical therapist who had helped me walk the length of the hospital corridor came over to comfort me. She leaned over, patted me on the shoulder, and said, "It's overwhelming for everyone the first time. You weren't expecting to have to use a brace and a walker." I had just walked for the first time since my spinal fusion, and at only 50 years old, I was feeling very overwhelmed.

Within three months I had healed nicely and was able to go off my medications. I was eager to get on with my life, but I didn't know that my greatest battle was still ahead of me. Six months after my back surgery, I began to have difficulty walking. My legs were both painful and numb, and it felt as if they could not support me. After a few tests at the neurologist's office, I was informed that I had an incurable progressive neuromuscular disease.

A few weeks later, I received a permanent brace for my ankle—not a small one, but a leather brace that came almost to my knee. And if that wasn't bad enough, I also had to wear corrective shoes. And they were about the ugliest things I'd ever laid eyes on. I resented the time it took me to put the brace on, not to mention the shoes and the stares from people when I went out in public. One of my ventures, however, proved rather enlightening. I drove to the post office to mail some letters. In order to keep my back and leg straight, I could not get out of my car without hitting the car next to me. I was becoming more frustrated by the minute, until I raised my head and looked over into the other car. I was startled to see that the driver had a trachea tube. Silently I prayed, "Lord, I believe I will keep the brace."

Due to the nature of my disease, there were days I tired easily and had muscle spasms in my legs. Having been an ambitious person all my life, I did not like the idea of having to pace myself, but in order to function well I had to take time out during the day to rest.

Little by little, I accepted my situation, but it did not come quickly or easily. First, I had to walk through the valley of grief and all its stages. I learned to let the tears flow when I needed to, and this helped me cope. On some days the frustration and anger were almost unbearable, and then depression would hit and make me feel absolutely alone. I had to learn to reach out and ask for help.

Eventually, I looked around me and saw what I had left instead of what I had lost. Having been a Christian for many years, I had often prayed but not with the sincerity that I prayed now. Instead, my prayer was neither fancy nor eloquent, but straight from the heart. In the dark hours of the night, many times I prayed, "Lord, I really need you." To my surprise, I felt the peace the Bible talks about, one that surpasses all understanding.

In small steps, I made the effort to redefine my life. Having been an artist for many years, I became serious about my work instead of thinking of it as a hobby. With my husband's help, I converted an old, rundown building into an art studio. I painted it blue and planted petunias in the window boxes. Sitting on the side of a mountain overlooking a lake, my studio became a place of peace and tranquility. During the lazy days of summer, I would open the door and windows and listen to the chirping birds, along with my favorite tape of Beethoven. Outside I saw the petals of my favorite roses, and sometimes I could smell the fragrance of wild honeysuckle in bloom. Somehow the music seemed sweeter than before. Maybe, I realized, this was the first time I had slowed down long enough to really listen.

My doctors advised me to save as much of my energy as I could, so I purchased a bright red scooter. It took me several tries before I was finally able to sit on it. I had to put aside all my obsolete ideas about mobility aids and accept that they could help me live a more productive life. Now I'm extremely grateful for my scooter and for the freedom it allows me.

Having this disease has taught me to listen to my body, to appreciate what it can and cannot do. I've also found that, regardless of what condition my body is in, I still have control of my state of mind.

A friend asked me recently, "Glenda, how are you getting along?"

I thought about his question for a minute, and then I answered him, "You know, this may be the most meaningful period of my life." He raised his eyebrows and looked at me quizzically. How could I tell him that the lessons I'd learned had been worth the struggle? How could I explain the ways my faith had been strengthened or how I'd come to live more fully and peacefully?

I noticed the puzzled look on my friend's face, and I remembered something my father had said to me: "Glenda, sometimes you have to learn lessons the hard way." At that moment, I knew he was right.

I regard everything as loss . . . in order that I may gain . . . the righteousness from God based on faith.

Philippians 3:8–9

Lord God, I'm grateful today for all that you have given me, and I rejoice in the blessing of life. Help me see how you intend to enrich my life by my losses; help me see them from an eternal perspective. I want to learn to relate to you and others on a deeper, more meaningful level because of my trials. Help me in this, I pray. Amen.

Why does God permit us to lose some of the good gifts he has bestowed on us? Why does he take some of them back from us? There is no one answer that fits all situations, but there is one reality about God that can help us trust him in spite of our loss: God always has our best interest at heart. If we trust that this is true, and we draw nearer to him (rather than pull away), the merciful reasons for his permitting our loss appear to us, one by one, like the stars, shining steadily in the heavens. Our disappointment, then, gives way to a deepening love for the one who watches over our lives more carefully than we can fully comprehend.

Dear God, in my struggle with losing things I hold dear, please help me. I long for your comfort and for a renewed sense of joy and gratitude for the good gifts you have given me. Help me focus on the things of eternal value and to praise you for each one. I'll start by thanking you for my salvation. All else may become lost, but my life belongs to you forever because you have found me and will always walk with me. I praise you for this!

I believe that I shall see the goodness of the Lord in the land of the living. Wait for the Lord; be strong, and let your heart take courage; wait for the Lord!

Psalm 27:13–14

Father, I take hold of you today. Grant me faith and confidence in your good plans for my life. Help me wait expectantly for you to show me the path of life today. I will count my blessings, find reasons to praise you, and walk in gratitude with you. Amen.

I lost my grandmother to cancer five years ago. She passed rather quickly. She was one of the most loving people I've ever met. At her memorial service, the theme of her life—unconditional love—emerged again and again in the testimonies of people who had known her. It wasn't the kind of love that ignores the truth, though; it was the kind that could look at the truth about you—the good and the bad—and love you still.

She never tried to impress anyone, and she did not care if she had nice things or not. She lived simply with one purpose: to love as God loves.

As I helped my aunt prepare Grandma's poems and memoirs for publication, I came to realize that during her life, she experienced loss—plenty of it: 110 acres of prime property on an island were essentially stolen from her; two husbands died as did two daughters; and she laid down her independence when she felt she could no longer drive. In all her years, however, I never once heard her complain about any of her losses, not even when the inevitability of her dying was apparent to her. She had her mind set on all that she stood to gain when she finally would meet the author of her faith, the lover of her soul, and the giver of all good gifts. She is my shining example of one who knew how to live with loss and yet rise far above it.

For what will it profit them if they gain the whole world but forfeit their life? Or what will they give in return for their life?

Matthew 16:26

Is anything ours that has not been given to us by God?
Our very life is a gift. We are not our own. Even the
things we have "earned" in life have come to us as a
result of the physical strength and mental capabilities
God has bestowed on our lives, and so every truly
good thing we have belongs to him. He grants us
good things, sometimes for a season, sometimes for
a lifetime, but always for our good and to his glory.
More than anything, he desires for us to have the thing
our spirits crave most: relationship with him. And,
thankfully, he won't let any gift stand in the way of that
supreme gift.

*For though the Lord is high, he regards
the lowly.... Though I walk in the
midst of trouble, you preserve me ... and*

your right hand delivers me. The Lord will fulfill his purpose for me; your steadfast love, O Lord, endures forever.

Psalm 138:6–8

Merciful God, you have poured out many good gifts on my life, and I thank you for each one. Thank you, too, for the gifts that you have given me only for a season. I acknowledge your right to give and to take away, and I even rejoice in it, because I know that you are always seeking to bless me. Help me trust your goodness and your love for me as you walk with me, now and always. Amen.

CHAPTER 4

Our Neediness: A Place to Meet God

*S*ince neediness can carry the stigma of weakness, we sometimes feel shame when we are in need. But true need is nothing to be ashamed of. God loves us, and he knows that we have deep spiritual needs that we can manage to ignore when we are physically comfortable. Our neediness, therefore, creates a meeting place for us with God, a place where we discover that we don't have to go it alone on our own strength, for God walks with us, providing for all our needs.

Even a Snickers Bar

In 1988, I was living in Arizona and was laid off from my designing job. Because I was a single parent of two children, Jonathan, 11, and Heather, 9, I had to find a way to provide for my family. After applying for unemployment, I was told that I would receive a mere $135 a week. My rent was $450 a month, and utilities were not included. Plus there were all the other day-to-day expenses to consider: groceries, gasoline, and so forth. I didn't know what we were going to do.

I cut our expenses any way I could. For instance, we ate a lot of potatoes and did our laundry by hand. The church gave us several boxes of groceries, but their food bank was running low.

There were other things besides food that Jonathan and Heather needed. School supplies and clothing were the main priorities, but I couldn't afford either. Both children attended a private Christian school, and the school had graciously allowed for our bill to be

paid at a later time. This was very kind of them, but
I knew it was another bill adding up to be paid
whenever money finally came in.

Around the third month, I made homemade burritos
with refried beans for the children to take for lunch
every day. Then in the evenings we had "make a
burrito" night. This went on for weeks. (To this day,
Heather will not eat a bean burrito!) Finally, by the
end of the third month, we were down to one
box of macaroni. We had no meat, no bread, no
vegetables . . . just a box of plain macaroni. The only
hope I had was to trust in God and pray. So I did.

It's funny how our prayers match our needs. For
three months I'd been praying for another job, for a
way to manage my money, and for the children to
have enough food to eat. Now, my prayers became
desperate. There were no more ingredients for
burritos, no refried beans, no food supply of any kind.
I was on my knees begging God to provide, and in the
midst of this earnest prayer I began to think about
Snickers candy bars. Snickers were my favorite candy
in the whole world—but how could I think of such an
extravagant treat at this time? I was embarrassed before

God and felt guilty for even thinking of something so ridiculous. I asked for his forgiveness and prayed that he would provide us with some healthy food.

That afternoon, I heard a knock on the door. When I opened it, there stood my dear friend Anita from church. She said she had been to a neighborhood prayer meeting that morning, and they had gathered up five bags full of groceries to donate to someone in need. Anita had suggested giving the groceries to me. She said she hoped there were things in the bags that we could use and enjoy. I told her that we were so delighted to have whatever was in there, we would use it all.

After Anita left, I started to go through the groceries. All the staples were included, plus some wonderful meats, vegetables, and fruits. Everything looked so delicious! And then I noticed it: a Snickers bar. But there wasn't just one bar—there was a whole bag of Snickers bars!

I couldn't help but cry. God cared for me so much that he not only provided the foods we needed but also supplied me with a treat I loved. I knew it was his way of letting me know he was going to be with us through it all and would take care of the children and me. I smiled, feeling my fears and anxieties being replaced by an unquestionable trust in God. I put the groceries away, said a prayer of thanks, then sat down and enjoyed a Snickers. I knew then that everything was going to be okay.

Father, today I embrace my neediness as part of who I am, as part of how you made me. I was made to need and to have my needs met by you. Help me not be ashamed of my God-given needs. I look to you and wait for your perfect provision. I give you thanks. In Jesus' name.

My God will fully satisfy every need of yours according to his riches in glory in Christ Jesus. To our God and Father be glory forever and ever. Amen.

Philippians 4:19–20

When I was in the fourth grade, the union my dad was part of went on strike for six months. For six months, my mom stretched our food budget. Crock-Pot cooking became her specialty. I remember eating lots of stew, navy bean soup, and spaghetti. Leftovers abounded, and we never went hungry. Today I realize that in my 37 years of living, I have never once been forced to go without a meal. The times I did go without were by choice, not by necessity. That's an amazing track record of God's goodness. And yet in all of those years of abundance, it is those six months of leanness that best highlight for me the provision I have always enjoyed from his faithful hand.

God, you are my provider. I want to look to you to meet my needs, whether you meet them supernaturally or in ordinary ways. Help me see and rejoice in your goodness to me. Help me not turn down your provision if it comes to me through others. I surrender my pride and my fear to you, as I trust your wisdom for my life. Amen.

Let us therefore approach the throne of grace with boldness, so that we may receive mercy and find grace to help in time of need.

Hebrews 4:16

Lord God, I have nothing to fear when I place my trust in you. You own all things. All good things for my life are in your hands to grant at the right time. Teach me to rest in the knowledge that you never withhold any good thing from those who walk with you in a spirit of uprightness.

Diapers

Laughing and chatting among ourselves, we milled around while catching up on the latest news. Though we met weekly, an outsider might have thought we hadn't seen one another in months. We were a close group of moms who deeply cared about one another. We'd gotten to know each other well by sharing personal experiences that bonded us.

Many of us met regularly, and others dropped by when they could, so the group was always changing, shifting, never quite the same. But whoever showed up was warmly welcomed and accepted, immediately becoming part of the group. So it was with Lisa, who had joined us fairly recently. Often late, usually breathless, as stressed as anyone we'd ever seen, Lisa had become one of us as thoroughly as if she'd been with us for years.

Now we all welcomed her as she burst through the door, breathing hard, hair flying in all directions, with her youngest child propped on one hip.

"Sorry," she apologized for the baby's presence. "I couldn't get a sitter at the last minute." She knew she'd be perfectly welcome, even if the baby got fussy and noisy. She began settling down, speaking to us about the chaos of her morning, the problems that had almost kept her away from the group.

We knew some of it: the recent, sudden divorce; the devastation she felt; the urgent stresses of raising a young family unexpectedly alone. But this day had hit her harder than most, draining her strength, her courage, her determination to make it work despite her loneliness and misery. She let the words pour out of her aching spirit, and we all listened intently.

"I don't know how I'll manage," she confided. "I just can't earn enough to keep us going. The bills are piling up, the rent's overdue, and the car needs work. I've prayed and prayed for strength, for faith, but I keep falling apart. I know God can provide for me and the kids. I just can't feel it in my heart. I keep feeling panicky, you know, like what am I going to do?"

Tears slid down her cheeks now, as the enormity of all she faced without her husband overwhelmed her. We moved close to give her hugs and support, murmuring encouraging words, promising prayer and all the help we could manage. None of us could do much. We were all familiar with the struggles of budget problems and financial crises.

"Oh," Lisa said softly, the discouragement still strong in her eyes. "I forgot... I had so little money, there wasn't even enough for basics. Sarah's wearing the last disposable diaper right now. I don't even have a change for her." There was such distress in her face.

I felt a shiver race along my spine, a shiver of awe and astonishment. I'd forgotten the sack tucked behind my chair, the sack I'd felt an impulse to grab at the last minute as I hurried from home to be on time for our group. I reached back behind the chair to pull it out. It was just a plain grocery sack, but my hand was shaking as I reached for it.

I held it out to Lisa. "Here," I told her. "My daughter doesn't wear these anymore. I brought them in case anyone could use them." Lisa pulled open the sack and stared inside, her face alight with the same astonishment I felt myself. She looked at us all, her eyes bright, a smile bursting across her features as she pulled out the sack's contents.

Inside was a large package of diapers in exactly the size her daughter needed. We knew immediately that God had heard our prayers and would provide for Lisa's needs, both large and small.

Therefore do not worry, saying, "What will we eat?" or "What will we drink?" or "What will we wear?" . . . your heavenly Father knows that you need all these things. But strive first for the kingdom of God and his righteousness, and all these things will be given to you as well.

Matthew 6:31–33

Lord, I need to know that you are near and tha...
When I focus on you and fix my attention on your suffu...
instead of on my needs, my fear fades and my faith rises up. I
want to live in that peace today. Meet me here, I ask.
In Jesus' name. Amen.

In his sermon on the mount, Jesus tells us to observe nature to get an idea of God's care for us. The sparrows have nests and food; the grass is clothed with lovely flowers. How much more significant are our lives to God than these things! He will not overlook our need for food, shelter, and clothing. The only thing that can keep us from his abundant provision is our refusal to seek him and to receive all that he has in store for us. And so as we turn from pride and self-sufficiency and walk in humility toward God's sufficiency, we find that we are no longer alone. Now we have a Father who delights to walk with us and who faithfully sees to each of our needs.

Blessed are the poor in spirit, for theirs is the kingdom of heaven. . . . Blessed are those who hunger and thirst for righteousness, for they will be filled.

Matthew 5:3, 6

Father, lift my eyes to see the joy of relationship with you regardless of what I cannot see right now in the way you provide for my physical needs. I rest this day in your promise that you will supply all of my needs—every single one of them—in Christ Jesus. In my neediness, you make a place for me to meet with you. Thank you for your desire to walk with me and for your power to provide. Amen.

CHAPTER 5

He Carries Our Cares

*W*orry, anxiety, frustration, tension, stress—these can eat us alive if we let them. But we don't need to let them if we understand that God helps us in times of trouble. God's love for his children includes his desire to carry our burdens, to give us rest in the middle of chaos, and to teach us the secret of peace in all circumstances. No matter what overwhelming situation we find ourselves in, God is still bigger. God is able to show himself strong on our behalf. Take heart today! God is with you and for you! You can find peace as you walk with him.

When Angels Kiss

As a little girl, my favorite Bible story was that of
Samuel, the boy who heard God's voice. I was only
about four years old the first time I heard it in Sunday
school, but I remember how badly I wanted to hear
God call my name, too. I would lie awake in bed,
straining my ears to filter out the night sounds of
ticking clocks, crickets, creaking floor boards, and my
father's snoring. I wondered what God's voice would
sound like. Would it be a booming shout or a quiet
whisper? Would I still be awake when he called to me,
or would it happen at night while I was sleeping? I
never imagined it would take 40 years to finally learn
the answers to my questions.

It was a beautiful Sunday morning in August, so clear
and free of humidity that the air sparkled. This day was
my 44th birthday. It was also the day my mother died.
She had been ill for only two weeks, and as a health
care worker, I knew what could have happened, so I
was grateful she went peacefully. But as her daughter, I

was tormented with thoughts that maybe there was something I had overlooked; something that, had I caught it in time, could have saved my mother.

That night was one of the hardest of my life. I found no solace in the company of others, though I knew my sister was grieving, too. All we had now was each other, and I felt terribly alone. I prayed through the night that God would help me, and although I didn't hear him answer, he did.

Over the following days, I worked on a tribute for the memorial service. Finding the right words was not difficult since Mom had been a strong Christian up to the end. But I knew I could add some special touches by looking in her Bible. She had always told me, "Remember, everything's written in here." I had never opened her Bible before because I thought of it as her personal property, like a pocketbook or a diary. Now I would have to look inside her Bible to find where she had noted her favorite hymns and passages. Afraid it would start me crying again, my hands trembled as I opened it. But my fear of sorrow dissolved as I read what she had written, and a blanket of peace began to settle over me.

Next to different verses, Mom had jotted down the names of family and friends, as happy reminders or promises to pray for them. In the margins were dates, observations, and the chronology of her Christian journey. I was surprised to learn she had become a Christian at the age of 44, the same age I turned the day she died. It was like the completion of a cycle for me, learning that we shared a "birthday" of sorts. What I didn't realize was that this whole time God was whispering in my ear; I just wasn't hearing him... yet.

As time passed, fear started poking through my sorrow. How was I going to pay all the bills and maintain the house on my own? What if a major appliance or the car broke down? What if I became sick or lost my job? I was giving a lot of public lip service to God, saying he would take care of me, but privately my worry was gnawing away at me.

Then, one morning on my way out the door, an object in the corner of the kitchen caught my eye: a little antique chalkboard. It had hung on the wall there for years, used for memos, grocery lists, and baking times. Taking it for granted, I hadn't noticed the words written on it before. Now the words nearly leapt off the old scratched slate. In my mother's handwriting, these words were written: "Jesus Is a Way Maker" and "Jesus Never Fails." My heart skipped a beat when I read them. I felt like Samuel! Through my mother, God had spoken to me, and I had finally heard him.

I resolved never to wipe my mother's words from the slate. They would remind me of God's presence, and from that day on, I started noticing other things that gave me pause and confirmed what I was slowly learning: God's voice is everywhere.

The following spring, I was walking down the driveway to the mailbox when I saw something shining among the stones and gravel. Thinking the object to be a piece of metal that had dropped from the recycling bin, I bent to pick it up. To my amazement, I found myself holding a pin of a small pair of praying hands. It had been my mother's, and I had lost it eight months prior on the day of her memorial service. It had been there through the winter, in rain and snow, driven over countless times. Yet, incredibly, here it was, shiny as new, safe in my palm, a reminder of God's love.

Less than a month later, I came home from work to find another curious sight. I had previously set some small porcelain cherubs on a chair by the back door. Now two of them had fallen over, one on its back, the other kneeling over it, their faces locked in a kiss. There was no wind; it had been a calm day. My first thought was "Mom." It was the playful sort of thing she would have done. My sister said the same thing when I described the little angels to her. "Mom visited you," she said.

Bluebirds, the traditional sign of happiness and good fortune, were always just a fleeting sight for us on their migratory route each spring and fall. But since my mom died, a family of four has lived in my yard year-round. There are no feeders or birdhouses to attract them, but every day I see a bit of bright blue cheer flitting in the trees and across the lawn. I think of them as another sign. To me, the birds represent my family—my parents, my sister, and myself—and they remind me that we'll all be together again one day.

Living in the country, I've always enjoyed the quiet nights, sitting outside watching the stars. There are times when I lose sight and forget my chalkboard's

messages. I feel sad when I can't afford a movie rental
on a Saturday night because there's only ten dollars
left between now and next payday. But then I'll see a
brilliant streak of light arc across the sky and remember
I'm not alone. Watching a magnificent meteor shower,
nature's fireworks, fills me with awe—and it's free!

What took me so long to learn was that the gift I'd
wanted for so many years had always been there. I just
wasn't ready to accept it. Now I know God's voice can
be heard at any time in a variety of ways, whether it's
loud as thunder or soft as an angel's kiss. All the things
I had filtered out were part of God's voice trying
to get in. His voice is like mixed-media artwork: a
symphony played to the northern lights wrapped in
a garden painted in gold. He's been talking to me all
along. But now I've learned to "listen" with all
my senses.

One day not too long ago, a beautiful, perfectly heart-
shape cloud drifted across the sky. I smiled as it passed
and whispered back, "I love you, too."

Holy Spirit, you fill my heart with peace and assurance in the middle of my troubles. Thank you for the gentle ways you tell me that you are taking care of me. Help me listen to your voice that says to my heart (just as Jesus said to the wind and the waves), "Peace, be still!" I want to rest knowing that you are walking close beside me today.

Do not worry about anything, but in everything by prayer and supplication with thanksgiving let your requests be made known to God. And the peace of God, which surpasses all understanding, will guard your hearts and your minds in Christ Jesus.

Philippians 4:6–7

God, I bring you each of my concerns this day. As I name them right now, help me release them into your care. As you carry them in your capable hands, I will leave them there and enjoy freedom from anxiety. Thank you for walking with me today and for being so attentive to the things that are on my mind. In Jesus' name. Amen.

Cast all your anxiety on him, because he cares for you.

1 Peter 5:7

That bill is due, and the money is not there. Your child is not home, and it's past the curfew. You need to make an important decision, but you have no idea what you should do. What stressful situation is staring you in the face right now? Don't be afraid to call on God. It's okay to be weak and needy; God is your strength and sufficiency. He wants to be there for you. He will come alongside you and show you the way to peace of heart and mind.

Father, the world is such an uncertain place. I realize that there is no real security outside of your care. That's why I'm grateful that you, the Almighty God, are the one who walks with me on this journey. I praise your name because nothing is too difficult for you.

God carefully knit you together in your mother's womb (see Psalm 139). As you consider the care with which you have been put together, trust that God also has a wonderful plan for your life. Circumstances may look chaotic to you right now. But the God who holds your life is the God who, at creation, spoke the order of the universe into the chaos of dark nothingness. Call on him. Run to him. He will show you the way when it seems there is no way. In his care you need never worry, for he will never leave you to walk alone.

The Lord is my shepherd. .
though I walk through the da. .
valley, I fear no evil; for you are with
me; your rod and your staff—they
comfort me.

Psalm 23:1, 4

Lord Jesus, as I walk with you, there is no cause for fear or
anxiety. Thank you for inviting me to be in this close
relationship with you. I lay down the concerns of my life right
now, knowing you will take care of each one in your time and
in your way—the way that is best for me. Help me walk
with peace in my heart and mind today as I place my hand
in yours. In your name. Amen.

CHAPTER 6

A Hero for the Helpless

*A*t the point where we become completely powerless to help ourselves, we are forced to surrender our lives to God's control. What happens from there is totally his call. And if we are uncertain of God's concern for us, it can be a scary thing. But the truth about God is that he is good, and he is willing and able to rescue us in our helplessness and to keep us safe from harm. His deepest desire, though, is to continue walking with us after the crisis has passed, guiding us and keeping us day by day so that we need never face those times of helplessness without him.

The Scenic Route

I set off in the early morning for my grandmother's house, giving myself plenty of time to arrive before lunch. The air was cold and crisp, signaling the change of seasons. Settling in for the long drive, I buzzed along the interstate, enjoying the colorful leaves. Usually I stick to the main highway, but with so much beautiful foliage to see and extra time on my hands, I turned off to parallel the turnpike.

The scenic road curved and wound its way through wooded hills and valleys. Sunlight glittered through the trees. I rounded a bend and crossed over a bridge, smiling with delight at the dazzling oak, maple, and ash trees all around me. It was a beautiful day for sightseeing, and I was anxious to share all the details of nature's glory and wonder with Grandma when I arrived for my visit.

Suddenly, I realized that a broad semitruck was barreling out of control and heading directly toward me. Its huge tires straddled the double yellow line. The truck crossed farther into my lane.

My heart raced as adrenaline flooded my body. I had only a split second to react. At the last possible moment, I whipped the wheel to the right to avoid a head-on collision. As I slammed on my brakes, the sickening smell of burnt rubber filled my nostrils. The rear end of the truck clipped the fender of my car, sending me headlong down into a ravine.

"Oh, Lord," I cried out in terror, "please help me!" The last thing I remember was hearing the scream of my own voice.

I didn't know what time it was when I came to, but the sun was high overhead. My head throbbed, and it took me a moment to remember how I'd ended up in my overturned car. The truck driver apparently had not stopped, for I was alone. Slowly I reached out to grasp the window frame, but a bolt of pain shot through my right arm.

I realized my arm was broken and tried not to panic when I saw it dangling in an unnatural position.

Wrapping my sweater around it was an effort, but it hid the injury. Again I tried to slide out of the wreckage, but my right lower leg was pinned. I was trapped. I tried to stay calm and think of a way out of my predicament. After a long while I heard the sound of a car approaching. The engine hummed, getting louder and louder as the car drew near. I felt a spark of hope.

"Help! Please, anybody! Help me!" My dry throat ached as I called out, but no one heard my cries. The car passed on the curve above and continued along the road, the sound of its engine growing fainter until it disappeared.

No one could see me down in the ravine, and I couldn't reach the road. My optimism turned into despair. It could be weeks before someone found me. The contents of my car were scattered everywhere. My cell phone wouldn't work down in this ravine even if I knew where it was. My auto insurance card, a map, a tissue box, and a small book of psalms lay at my side. I picked up the book with my left hand and opened it. The first thing I saw was Psalm 31:5—"Into your hand I commit my spirit. . . ."

"No!" I cried. "I'm not ready to die. I have so much to live for!"

I flipped to a different page and saw Psalm 116:1—"I love the Lord, because he has heard my voice and my supplications." Then I read Psalm 116:3–4—"The snares of death encompassed me;...I suffered distress and anguish. Then I called on the name of the Lord: 'Oh Lord, I pray, save my life!'"

How perfect the verses were, as though the Lord had read my heart. The words inspired me and gave me hope. I closed my eyes tightly and prayed, calling on the Lord with all my heart and soul, asking for a miracle.

The afternoon passed, and the sun moved lower in the sky. The air started getting chilly. Soon it would be dark. I clung to the hope that somehow I would get out of there alive, but realistically I knew that I might end up dying there. I cried bitter tears for all the lost dreams I would not be able to fulfill. I sobbed when I thought of leaving my family behind. And then I cried out of self-pity.

A hand touched my shoulder lightly, and I jumped in alarm.

"Hey—it's all right," a soothing voice said. "Help is on the way."

I blinked twice to be sure it wasn't my imagination. "Are you for real, or am I dreaming?" I asked the young man standing outside my car.

"Yes, we're really here," he assured me. "We heard you crying when we were walking by."

"Walking by?" I asked in amazement. "We're out in the middle of nowhere. How could you be walking by?"

"My friend and I were driving along, and we ran out of gas about 200 feet down the road," he said, pointing over his shoulder with his thumb. "We were walking to the next town when we heard you crying. We thought it must be a hurt animal so we decided to investigate. Then we saw your car." His eyes swept across the ruined auto then back to me. "Lonnie is on his way to town to call an ambulance. We'll get you out of here," he said reassuringly.

His name was Mike Wells, and he was a student from the University of Oklahoma. He and his friend, Lonnie Turner, had taken this road on a whim to see the beautiful fall foliage. *What if they hadn't come this way? I thought. What if they hadn't run out of gas? And how did they happen to come here, on this very stretch of road?* The coincidence was too unbelievable. In the distance a siren blared, growing louder as it neared. I closed my eyes in amazement and offered a prayer of thanks to God.

I glanced down at my book of psalms, still clutched tightly in my hand, and read chapter 31, verse 2— "Incline your ear to me; rescue me speedily." I knew the Lord had sent me help and saved me from certain death.

As I rode in the ambulance to the hospital, I read one last verse, Psalm 118:1—"O give thanks to the Lord, for he is good; his steadfast love endures forever!" Knowing that the Lord had miraculously rescued me, I thanked him again and again.

Lord Jesus, I'm thankful that you watch over my life. When I have no place to turn for help, I have you. I always have you. And you are the best place to turn for help. Thank you for hearing my cries and for rescuing me. What would I do without you? You are the one who saves me when no one else can!

For I, the Lord your God, hold your right hand; it is I who say to you, "Do not fear, I will help you."

Isaiah 41:13

Mighty God, you have delivered me from situations for which I had no answers or resources. You are the one who helps the helpless. Please teach me to wait on you when I don't know what to do. Remind me in my helplessness that you will always open up the path before me and help me see it and walk on it. And best of all, you always walk with me. I give you praise! In Jesus' name. Amen.

Our soul waits for the Lord; he is our help and shield. Our heart is glad in him, because we trust in his holy name.

Psalm 33:20–21

It comes as a surprise to some that the quote "God helps those who help themselves" is not found in the Bible. So it might come as a relief for some of us to realize that, in our helplessness, God is not a toe-tapping parent who stands over us, telling us to buck up and get with it.

We came into the world helpless, and God provided parents and/or guardians to feed us, clothe us, change us. And even as adults, we are still helpless in many ways; we cannot even draw our next breath without God granting us the gift of life. So next time we are at the end of our rope and we call out to him for help, we can be confident that he will not respond by telling us to figure it out ourselves. Instead, he will come, in love, to give us the help we need.

Lord, I know that some of the predicaments I get myself in are of my own making. That's when I feel most reluctant to call on you for help. But, in spite of this, please grant me faith to believe that you want to help me. And although you want me to learn from my mistakes, you will not abandon me to be swallowed up by the consequences of them. Thank you for promising to be with me and for showing me how to make it as I grow through the process. I welcome your help today.

Take a moment to contemplate how big the world is and how fragile our bodies are. What a miracle that we are able to move about in such a world and survive one day in it! It would seem that we are far more helpless than we often realize and that God is far more involved in taking care of us than we may be able to comprehend. In humility and love he works behind the scenes in our lives, granting us tremendous help and provision. These gifts are worthy of our ongoing thanks and praise, because he has not left us to walk alone in this world.

God is our refuge and strength, a very present help in trouble. Therefore we will not fear.

Psalm 46:1–2

Father, I love that you call me your child. It helps me see the true nature of my relationship with you. I need you in so many ways. When I'm helpless, teach me not to feel ashamed ... just as children who have loving and attentive parents are not ashamed of asking for what they need. I confess my helplessness today as a gift from you that allows me to experience your strong and capable parental love for me.

My car had become stranded alongside the road, and I had called my dad to come pick me up. I didn't want anyone else's help. Only my dad would do in this situation. There is something strong and reassuring about his presence. He makes it seem as if everything will be okay. I never hesitate to call on him, and he never makes me feel ashamed or embarrassed when I'm helpless and need him.

Maybe that's one reason it is easy for me to see God, my heavenly Father, as a willing rescuer... a hero, so to speak. Of course, there are times when even my dad can't give me the help I need because he is limited like every human being. But God has never been stumped by my helplessness. He has never failed to rescue me when I've needed him. He is the Father of fathers.

I lift up my eyes to the hills—from where will my help come? My help comes from the Lord, who made heaven and earth. He will not let your foot be moved; . . . The Lord is your keeper.

Psalm 121:1–3, 5

Heavenly Father, I'm grateful that you see my helplessness, and you move in quickly to help me whenever I call on you. Forgive me for the times my pride has gotten in the way of receiving the help you offer me. Cause me to become more confident that you want to help me. I praise you for showing me that in my helplessness, I never walk alone, for you are my rescuer, my hero. Amen.

CHAPTER 7

When We Fail, God Stands by Us

*F*ailure—ours and others'—can be difficult to accept. When we fail, we are often disappointed and even disgusted with ourselves. How could we be so weak, so inept, so foolish? We may even assume that God feels the same way about us. But his Word reveals a different response: No matter how we may mess up, God continues to love us and longs to help us get back on our feet. What a relief! God doesn't turn away from us when we fail; he rushes to our aid and encourages us to try again. His mercy eases our pain, and his forgiveness offers a new start.

A Gift of Love

Jane Nelms awoke the morning of August 29, 1975, at her parents' house in Denver, Colorado, with severe labor pains.

"It's time," she told her mother.

She knew what her mother must be thinking. She could hear the words echo in her mind to the same percussion of pain and guilt she had felt since she married Chad. "You should not have gotten married, and this baby is a big mistake."

Jane's mother didn't like Chad or the fact that he had moved out of the young couple's apartment when Jane was six months pregnant. And she didn't think Jane was ready to have a child at age 19.

After Chad left, the company that employed Jane went out of business. She had no choice but to return to her parents' home. She knew she had failed her family by making poor choices. They loved her, but she didn't think she deserved their love—or God's. Not she, who had been rejected by her husband. She was unworthy.

After the labor pains began, Jane called Chad at the gas station where he worked.

"Please, Chad, come to the hospital with me," she begged him.

"It's your baby," he said. "I don't care about it."

Over and over, she pleaded with him to come. He refused. By the time Jane arrived at the hospital with her mother and sister, she was an emotional wreck. She was embarrassed to be there without a supportive husband. She felt worthless, like a failure, facing a future that looked as bleak as a barren plain.

After Jane was wheeled to the labor room, two nurses appeared. One of them was heavyset, middle-aged, average height, with a calm, soothing voice. Her name tag identified her as Mary. She looked motherly and huggable, and her presence made Jane feel safe.

Mary soon dismissed the other nurse by saying, "I can handle things from here."

Standing beside Jane in a white uniform, her dark hair a contrast to her light complexion, Mary asked, "Have you taken birthing classes?"

"No," Jane replied, thinking that was one more thing she had failed to do.

Mary taught Jane how to breathe so she could deal with the pain. Jane loved her calm voice, so different than the raised voices often used by her family.

By 4:00 P.M., Jane's labor pains had intensified. About that time, Chad arrived with his parents, who had forced him to come.

Mary had to tend to her other patients, but she popped in frequently to check Jane's pulse and blood pressure. When the nursing shift changed later that evening, Mary didn't go home. She stayed to be with Jane.

By 11:00 P.M., Jane was fully dilated, so she went to the delivery room. Chad went, too. He stood on Jane's left side, and Mary stood to her right. She explained everything that was happening. She tried to get Jane to push. But things weren't going well. The baby's heartbeat began to weaken. Someone gave Jane an epidural. But then she got sick, and she threw up. She needed oxygen, but she fought the oxygen mask, afraid she would throw up again and choke. Finally, Mary leaned close to Jane's face and whispered in her soothing voice, "You need to do this. The baby needs it." Mary's voice helped Jane calm down enough to accept the mask.

"Your baby is fine," Mary kept reassuring her. "You just need to keep breathing."

Mary didn't seem to care about the circumstances that had brought Jane to this place. She wasn't concerned about whether or not Jane had made a wise decision to marry and get pregnant right away. Her focus was on Jane and how she was doing. Mary continued to assure Jane that she would be all right.

"They don't think there's enough room for the baby to come," she explained later. "The doctors are trying to decide if they should take you up to surgery." Mary told Jane that a doctor had been contacted who could perform a cesarean section. Her calming voice helped Jane to relax.

When they wheeled Jane into the operating room, Chad was not allowed to go with her. But Mary never left her side.

Michelle was born at 1:30 A.M. on August 30.

After the other nurses had cleaned Michelle up, Mary asked Jane, "Do you want to see your baby girl?"

Jane looked into her daughter's eyes and examined her perfect features. "She's beautiful," Jane whispered. After spending some time with her new daughter, she handed the baby back to Mary and drifted off to sleep.

When Jane awoke in the recovery room, Mary was gone. Jane was in the hospital five more days, but she never saw Mary again.

After she recovered enough to return to her parents' house, Jane wrote thank-you notes to everyone who had helped her. She addressed the thank-you note to Mary to Aurora Community Hospital, thinking it would be delivered to her. But several days later, it came back with a note that no such person was at that address.

Jane telephoned the hospital's maternity ward. "A nurse named Mary helped me through a difficult labor," she explained. "I would like to thank her."

"No one by that name works here," the nurse said. "But occasionally we do hire temporary workers. Perhaps she was just a temp."

After Jane got off the phone, she thought more about Mary. Could she have been an angel? *Impossible,* Jane thought. She had fallen too far from God, made too many bad choices. God couldn't love her enough to send an angel. There had to be some other explanation.

But the more she thought about it, the more Jane realized that she had truly been given a gift when Michelle was born: a gift of love and forgiveness, and the presence of a kind soul who walked with her through a troubled, frightening time in her life. Mary didn't judge Jane. She didn't criticize her. She didn't remind her of the mistakes she'd made or the distance she had put between herself and God. All she cared about was helping Jane and assuring her that she and her baby would be fine.

If God had orchestrated all of that, Jane decided, then he really did love her. He didn't judge her. He didn't blame her for making poor decisions. He didn't care about any of that—he just cared about her. He cared enough to remind her that she was worthy of love, that she had not been abandoned. And he showed her all those things through the angelic presence of a nurse named Mary.

Lord Jesus, you see my weakness and, rather than turn away from me, you come to me and offer to be my strength. It encourages my heart to know that you are not ashamed of me and that you will never reject me. So next time I fail, help me not hide from you but instead call out to you for the help, forgiveness, and the healing I need. I'm so glad to know that you will always stand by me.

Poor Peter! He was the disciple of Jesus who had been most adamant about his commitment to stay with Jesus to the bitter end. And yet . . . when the heat was turned up, Peter bailed out, denying that he even knew Jesus.

Now Jesus was buried, and Peter had to live with the guilt of his denial. He had failed Jesus in his hour of need. Perhaps Peter thought that he didn't even deserve to be called a disciple. But Jesus thought differently. After Jesus had risen from the dead and the angel appeared to the women at the tomb, the angel said to the women, "You are looking for Jesus the Nazarene, who was crucified. He is not here. . . . tell his disciples and Peter . . ." The message from the angel was intended to assure Peter that he had not been rejected. His failure hadn't disqualified him from being counted among Jesus' followers. Jesus loved Peter.

And Jesus loves you. It doesn't matter how you've failed him; he wants to be in relationship with you.

❖━━━━◆━━━━❖

Our steps are made firm by the Lord, when he delights in our way; though we stumble, we shall not fall headlong, for the Lord holds us by the hand.

Psalm 37:23–24

Lord God, thank you for the lessons I have learned through my failures. Thank you for being with me and faithfully teaching me with love and understanding. You have never left me alone even at my worst moments. Your commitment to my life gives me the courage to keep trying. I'm so glad I belong to you.

Thomas Edison had many more failures than successes in his quest to bring electricity to the world. Yet, every failure whispered a bit more of the secret to success into his ear. The world is grateful that Edison did not curse his failures and quit trying. What secrets of success are your failures revealing to you today? What light is being shed on your future by them? God will come alongside you and open your understanding so that failure becomes a respected teacher rather than a dreaded enemy.

*Even youths will faint and be weary,
and the young will fall exhausted; but
those who wait for the Lord shall renew
their strength, they shall mount up with
wings like eagles; they shall run and not
be weary, they shall walk and not faint.*

Isaiah 40:30–31

*As I see my failures from your perspective, God, I see how they
help me walk closely with you. Help me not become defeated
when I sin or make mistakes; help me come to you with my
weakness so that I can receive your strength and
encouragement. Thank you for never giving up on me, for not
being ashamed of me, and for always being there for me. I'm
so blessed to belong to you because you always stand with
me. With you, I never walk alone. Amen.*

CHAPTER 8

A Friend to the Lonely

Even when people surround us, we can feel very lonely. We want to be known, understood, and accepted. We can be crying out for companionship while we pretend to be just fine on the outside. In whom can we find a friend like the one we secretly long for? Only in Jesus, who made us. He knows us intimately, understands us thoroughly, and accepts us unconditionally. Let the message of this chapter encourage you to invite Jesus into your loneliness so that his faithful friendship might bring comfort to you. For he promises to walk alongside us even in life's loneliest places.

Friday Nights

At 25, Jeannie Moore thought her life was over. She had married young, divorced young, and was living with her parents again. We were meeting over coffee to talk about her recent decision to ask Christ into her life. Jeannie had stumbled upon our church while jogging, then tiptoed to a back pew out of curiosity. Our pastor delivered a powerful sermon on the mercy of God, and one passage struck Jeannie's heart. It touched her so much that at the end of the service she asked if someone could teach her about having Jesus in her life. Her life-altering verse was Matthew 11:28: "Come to me, all you that are weary and are carrying heavy burdens, and I will give you rest."

After listening to her, I could understand why she wanted rest. She still loved her ex-husband, who had remarried, and it was tormenting her. Stalking him had become routine. I chose my words carefully. "Jeannie, I know God can give you a far better life, and I'm going to ask you to trust me on that." She stared into my eyes, looking desperately for something that would persuade her to believe me.

I started again, "What's the worst part of being divorced?" She quietly and sadly responded, "The loneliness; that's why I moved in with my parents."

"Is it helping?"

"My parents were young when they had me, so they're cool. I can come and go when I want." She fumbled for an example and finally remarked, "I had a date last week. When the guy picked me up, my dad told him to keep me out as late as he wanted and invited him back to use our hot tub." She grinned. Trying not to show my dismay over her father's remarks, I managed a half-smile and asked how the date went.

"So-so."

"Jeannie, do you think you need a man in order to be happy?" I felt I was losing her. "Lots of single people come to church hoping to meet someone to fill a gap in their lives, and sometimes that happens. But I believe that God wants to be first in your life. He wants you to have a happy, complete life—and it may not include a man." Jeannie crumpled her napkin and reluctantly agreed to consider the idea. I knew she was still hoping a man would be part of the solution.

"When is your loneliest time?"

"Friday nights. Every Friday night my husband and I went out to dinner. Our favorite spot was Red Lobster. He takes her there now."

"Then let's do something on Friday night." Jeannie hated the idea, I could tell. But I wasn't backing down.

"Anything in particular that you would like to do?" Jeannie asked dismally.

"How about a movie?" I beamed. "I'll call you Thursday." With that we pushed in our chairs and left. Jeannie was probably off to peek into her ex-husband's mailbox. I was going to pray. I needed God to show me some common ground that Jeannie and I could build on. Learning to trust me would help Jeannie learn to trust him.

Friday after work, I picked her up for an early movie, and then we went to a great Mexican restaurant. Over guacamole, I told her how my parents hadn't allowed me to go to movies when I was little because they "weren't appropriate for Christians to see." She was flabbergasted.

"When did you finally go?"

"When I was in college. I prayed about it a lot. But now I've come to know God in a more loving way than I think my parents did. Anyway, I don't think it's going to keep me out of heaven. . . . You don't want to know how old I was when I started wearing jewelry!"

"Jewelry?"

"Yep. Old-fashioned Methodists don't wear it. I figured I was lucky. The Amish can't even wear buttons!" Not wanting to dishearten her, I added, "I've found that God is much more interested in our hearts than in our buttons." That was our religion class for the evening. After we paid the check, I dragged Jeannie to an all-night drugstore.

First we went to the card department and read silly cards until our stomachs hurt from laughing. Next we tried on every pair of sunglasses they had, giggling at how ridiculous we looked with the price tags hanging over our noses. Our laughter began to attract a suspicious employee. I asked him which looked better on Jeannie, the hi-tech silver or the neon pink. He barely looked old enough to work, but he had a knack for customer service. "Put the pink ones on again," he told Jeannie. After she obliged, he remarked, "They look *good*." Good had about three syllables.

Jeannie blushed and put the impulse purchase into our shopping cart. The sales associate moved on; he was pushing a two-wheeler stacked with boxes. I grabbed Jeannie's shoulder and pointed to the printing on the boxes. They were filled with Dove Bars, and not the kind you wash with!

After we each got a double chocolate ice cream bar, we plopped on the curb and started to eat, wiping chocolate from each other's chins. When I spit on my napkin to get a big blob off her cheek, Jeannie laughed. "I can't believe you just did that! You spit on a handkerchief and wiped my face! Did you do that to your kids? I bet you did!"

"I swore I would never do it, but I guess I did."

"You're not old enough to be my mother, but it felt really momlike."

"Look, little charmer! I am old enough to be your mother and then some. I was at Woodstock."

"So was I!" she shrieked. I stared at her, then realized she meant Woodstock 1999. Dripping with chocolate, we sat on the curb comparing the groups we had seen and the antics of the crowds.

When I dropped her off, Jeannie was in great spirits. Before she got out of the car, she said, "Thank you—it felt good not to be sad."

On Sunday, she sat next to me in church. My husband was in the choir, so I usually sat alone. I rejoiced inwardly as Jeannie followed along in the Bible I had given her. After the service, I persuaded her to join my Bible study group over lunch at a nearby restaurant. Jeannie seemed happy to come along—until we said grace. She squirmed until I finally elbowed her gently to stop.

Everyone went back to their conversations. I slid out to go to the washroom, and when I returned, I was

careful to choose another place to sit. Jeannie looked
startled, giving me that "please don't abandon me"
look. I ignored her, knowing she'd have more fun
sitting next to Tracy, who was a solid Christian much
closer to her age. By the end of lunch, the two of them
were making golf plans, and I was feeling pretty smug.

My smugness came and went during the next year.
Sometimes Jeannie soared, and sometimes she
miscalculated the intensity of her pain. I became her
spiritual mentor and Bible study teacher. She became
part of our family and a major part of our church.
She stumbled, she grew, she read her Bible. Mostly,
she learned to love the Lord. Amazingly, after a few
months, she even said grace at the restaurant.

Jeannie is on the road to becoming whole again, and
she's already happier than she was in her marriage. In
time, she would like to meet someone, but not to fill
her life; she wants someone to complement her life.
God has lavished her with grace. He's shown her
mercy, and he has given her the gift of prayer.

During Lent, Jeannie hosted our World Day of Prayer
service. This worldwide women's event, held on the

first Friday in March, started decades ago. Jeannie was the perfect person to pick up the torch in our church, and she worked hard to promote the service anywhere she could. I had tears in my eyes when she stood in front of hundreds of women—on what would have once been a lonely Friday night—and led us in a prayer for the world.

Lord, forgive me for not always trusting that you know what I need when I am lonely. Help me open myself up to the opportunities you bring into my life for friendship. Please give me the courage to respond to others when they want to get to know me. I don't want to be alone, but sometimes it's hard to step outside of my comfort zone. I can do this, though, because no matter what happens, I will never be truly alone. You always walk with me.

The Lord is a stronghold for the oppressed, a stronghold in times of trouble. And those who know your name put their trust in you, for you, O Lord, have not forsaken those who seek you.

Psalm 9:9–10

Jesus, thank you that you see into my heart, into my need for companionship with others. Thank you that you are not too busy to notice me. You are not too pressed by other concerns to hear my heart's cry for a friend. Please bring close friends into my life who are devoted to you. I want you to be at the center of my most meaningful relationships. Thank you for walking with me, whether I have many friends or few.

*For you, O Lord, are my hope, my trust,
O Lord, from my youth. Upon you I
have leaned from birth; . . . Do not cast
me off in the time of old age; do not
forsake me when my strength is spent.*

Psalm 71:5–6, 9

*Father, you are with me. Help me be able to grasp that reality,
to take hold of it, and to know what it means that no matter
where I go, your presence is there. You are the most faithful of
friends. You are the most attentive listener. You are the one
who sees every tear and wants to comfort me. You care about
every aspect of my life. Loneliness will not be able to find a
resting place in my life when I understand that I need
never walk alone.*

God knows our need for relationships. His desire is for us to enjoy both aspects of companionship: relationship with him and relationship with other people. But even though he designed us for both, there can be times in our lives when we are hard-pressed to find human friendships. It is then that we come to understand how vital our relationship with God truly is.

We can survive for a time without others, but we cannot survive without God in our lives. Even when we have companions we care very much about, we instinctively know that something vital is missing if we have neglected our relationship with God. When we are feeling lonely, our relationship with God is the first place we can go to receive comfort and hope. God desires to give us meaningful relationships with others. We can trust him to work in our lives to bring these relationships about. In the meantime, we do not need to walk in loneliness, for God is walking with us.

Father of orphans and protector of widows is God in his holy habitation. God gives the desolate a home to live in.

Psalm 68:5–6

Lord God, thank you for creating me to be in relationship with you and with others. As friendships change and people come and go in my life, I thank you that you remain steady, your love unchanging. Teach me to walk in close relationship with you so that loneliness does not overwhelm me at times when I feel alone. Help me realize that as long as you are with me, I don't need to be afraid of being alone. And as long as I live, you promise to walk with me. I praise you for that!

CHAPTER 9

Abandoned but Not Forsaken

*T*he pain of abandonment leaves us full of fear about the future and deeply insecure about our worth. And once this trust is shattered, we often—because we have been wounded—push away the very thing we need most: eternal, unconditional love. When we are dealing with the pain of abandonment, we may not notice the steady, strong, unchanging love of God as he reaches out to support us, offering comfort, hope, and healing. Yet, his love is real. It is gentle as it soothes and powerful as it restores.

Christmas Cookies

It was only two days before Christmas, and Sheena didn't know what to do. She looked at her six sleeping children. Her son was the oldest at age six, then came the four-year-old twins, and lastly the one-year-old triplets.

She sighed, thanking God for them. She loved her babies, but she was tired. Their father was gone—he did not want the responsibility—so she was left to raise six children by herself on a $700-a-month income. Sometimes it felt like too much for her to handle.

"Mommy," her son had asked recently, "are we going to get any toys this year?"

"I don't know, honey. I hope so."

"Is Daddy coming?"

"I don't know, sweetheart," Sheena said, trying to hold back her angry tears.

When her husband had first started to disappear after the twins were born, Sheena should have known what to expect. But he always came back with whispers of love, and she would hope that this time would be different.

Then she became pregnant again. When the doctor said they had another set of twins on the way, that was it. He finally left for good. Three kids were enough to handle, but with two more coming at the same time again, he ran scared, not wanting to share in the awesome responsibility.

Sheena was alone for the whole difficult term, but when it was time for the babies to be born, she managed to track down her husband through a cousin. He made it just as they were preparing her for a C-section.

During the birth, to everyone's surprise, including the doctors', the nurses', and Sheena's, they found another baby. That had been the problem during her entire pregnancy: None of them knew about the third baby.

Sheena was shocked, elated, and devastated all at the same time. She wept with tears of joy and uncertainty as she looked at her three precious boys.

Needless to say, their daddy left a few days later, and Sheena was left to raise three newborn babies along with the children they already had.

"I can't do it anymore, Lord," she cried quietly into her pillow so as not to wake the children. "Now with Christmas coming, it's too much for me to handle."

Suddenly the window shook, drawing her attention to the frosty windowpane. Sheena sat up and opened the blinds. Snow was falling quietly in the night. A gust of wind reminded her that they could be out in the street, cold and hungry.

Pulling the ragged but warm cover to her chin, Sheena said a prayer of thanks: Each child had their own bed, pajamas, and warm covers, and on the dresser three full bottles of milk were ready for the triplets' first feeding in the night.

"Lord, I'm sorry. I know I'm blessed. We've got our health, we've got food, and so far I can pay the rent and the heat bill. And, most of all, I've got six babies who love me." Sheena sighed and closed her eyes. "I'm sorry," she whispered again before falling asleep.

The next morning, the phone rang. "Hey!" It was her mother. "Listen, I got some things for my grandbabies. I'll bring them over later. And don't forget about Christmas dinner—we're expecting all of you to join us."

Sheena hung up, thanking God for all the help her mother and stepdad had given her. The phone rang again. She wondered if her mother had forgotten something.

"Hello," an unfamiliar voice said. "You might not remember me, but I'm one of the nurses that helped deliver your three miracle babies."

"Oh," Sheena replied, a little surprised. "What can I do for you?"

"Several of us nurses got together and bought gifts for your six children. I was wondering when we could drop them off."

After a moment of silence, the nurse said, "Hello? Are you still there?"

"Yes," Sheena finally answered with a quavering voice. She couldn't believe this was happening. She arranged for the nurse to stop by the next afternoon during nap time. That way, she could hide the gifts.

As soon as she hung up, the doorbell rang. Peeking outside, Sheena saw a smiling woman with a bag in each arm. Cracking the door open, she looked at the lady and noticed a man behind her standing near their open car door.

"Can I help you?" Sheena asked.

"Hi, sweetie," the woman said. "We're from the Methodist church, and we heard about your triplets from one of the interns at the hospital. The church is donating food for you and your children for the holiday."

With her mouth open and tears threatening to spill over, Sheena nodded, and the couple brought in six bags and two boxes, depositing them on the kitchen floor. "Thank you," was all she could manage to say.

As the woman walked out the door, she pressed an envelope into Sheena's hand. "God bless you, and have a merry Christmas," she said.

The three older children squealed excitedly as they peeked in the bags. Sheena set the envelope on the counter.

"Mommy, too-tees?" one of the four-year-olds asked.

"What, baby?" Sheena asked, wiping the tears from her eyes.

"Too-tees, Mommy," the child replied, pointing to a bag of cookies.

After seating the older three with cookies and milk, Sheena gave each of the triplets a bottle. Then she stole a minute to run to the bathroom and lay her head on the cool edge of the sink.

She finally burst with all the emotion that had been building up. It never failed—just when she felt as though she couldn't take it anymore, God sent a miracle to say, "Hold on a little while longer. I do understand."

Wiping her face with a washcloth, Sheena smiled and went back to her little angels. "I love you," she told each of them.

"We love you, too, Mommy," they said happily, cookie crumbs around their mouths.

Sheena looked at the bags, boxes, and envelope, then smiled again as she looked at her children. It was going to be a great Christmas after all.

Be strong and bold; have no fear or dread...because it is the Lord your God who goes with you; he will not fail you or forsake you.

Deuteronomy 31:6

Lord Jesus, you understand what it feels like to be abandoned, for your closest friends left you in your hour of greatest need. You know what my pain feels like, and you care for me. Thank you for hearing me when I call out to you from my place of need and for answering me.

If my father and mother forsake me, the Lord will take me up. . . . I believe that I shall see the goodness of the Lord in the land of the living.

Psalm 27:10, 13

As she stood in the church parking lot, Jana's eyes pooled with tears. Her parents had left without her. From her eight-year-old perspective, she wondered, *How could they?* How could they not notice that she was not among the other kids who had been ferried to church in her family's station wagon? Sure there were lots of kids to keep track of, but Jana wasn't just

113

anyone, she was their daughter! The fact of not being missed, of not being noticed translated to her heart as not being important, not being significant. It stung to be abandoned, even if it wasn't intentional.

Abandonment—on a large or small scale—has that effect on the human heart. It injures our sense of worth and undermines our security. There is only one place where our worth and security cannot be threatened, and that is at the center of the relationship with the one who loves us most. When we derive our significance from his estimation of our worth and we anchor our sense of security in his love, we will never feel abandoned.

Father, thank you for filling my heart with the knowledge that you truly love me. Help me not allow my changing circumstances and emotions to dictate how I will respond to your unchanging love. Cause me to stand in faith today that what you say—not how I feel—is the truth. And the truth is that I am your child, and you promise to be with me always.

The element of betrayal in abandonment is formidable. Someone we considered a friend deals us a treacherous blow. There is no way to get around the pain of it. So where do we find the comfort and help we need to heal from this kind of hurt? There is one who has experienced the wounds of betrayal and abandonment and yet did not give in to bitterness and hatred. Jesus was betrayed by a friend, abandoned by his followers, and left alone to die. He is the one who can teach us the way of forgiveness. Though it may seem impossible to us right now, Jesus is a gentle healer who can release us from the bitterness of betrayal and the fear of abandonment so that we can trust and love again.

When the righteous cry for help, the Lord hears, and rescues them from all their troubles. The Lord is near to the brokenhearted, and saves the crushed in spirit.

Psalm 34:17–18

115

Lord, your promises are sometimes hard to hang on to. Others have broken their promises to me, and so sometimes it's a struggle to trust in anything or anyone. But you don't lie and you don't change, so help me lay down my wariness and move toward you in faith. Every time I talk to you, I know you're there. Thank you for being so faithful to me.

Doors don't need to slam shut behind someone exiting our lives for us to feel the wounds of abandonment. The pain of being *emotionally* shut out of a loved one's life is every bit as real as being physically left alone by them. When emotional doors get closed in our face, the only way to gain access again is by permission of the one who closed the door in the first place. We are at their mercy, and there is no guarantee that they will ever open the door again.

The hurt of being shut out, however, is not something we need to deal with alone. God himself knows our heartache, for he is often left on the outside of the very hearts he has created. As he holds us in his love, he is able to comfort us and protect us from the poison of resentment and bitterness. He also teaches us how to keep our own heart open to those who have shut us out. Best of all, he remains with us as we wait in hope to be invited back into relationship with them.

Where can I go from your spirit? . . . If I ascend to heaven, you are there; if I make my bed in Sheol, you are there. If I take the wings of the morning and settle at the farthest limits of the sea, even there your hand shall lead me, and your right hand shall hold me fast.

Psalm 139:7–10

Just as the birds begin to stir and sing before dawn has broken, so God's Spirit begins to stir our hearts with hope of healing and renewal as the darkness of abandonment fades. He helps us lift our prayers in faith and makes us able to believe again that there are friends who will be faithful and relationships that will bring us joy. And as we realize that the night is passing, the Spirit of God readies us for a new day, putting praise in our hearts and a song on our lips.

Jesus said, "And I will ask the Father, and he will give you another Advocate, to be with you forever. This is the Spirit of truth. . . . he abides with you, and he will be in you."

John 14:16–17

Sometimes when we feel abandoned by our friends and family, they really haven't abandoned us. It just seems as if they have. Other times, for some of us, our loved ones have abandoned us, and that can be very painful. What is far worse is when we feel abandoned by God. But despite how we feel, God will never leave our side—that we can be sure of.

Jesus, you are Immanuel—God with us. I know that you tasted abandonment for my sake so that I need never walk alone. Thank you for caring about me so much that no obstacle, not even death, will ever get in the way of your love for me. Please heal my heart with your love so I can embrace others without fear, for I trust in you to walk with me now and forever. Amen.

CHAPTER 10

Kept Safe in Danger

*W*e live in a dangerous world, but Jesus told his followers to take heart because he has overcome this world. As God's children, we are not at the mercy of chance nor are we victims of the whims of evil. God permits only trials that will help us grow strong in faith, and he will not allow anything to cut short the number of days he has determined for our lives. Our heavenly Father walks with us through danger, and his protective presence keeps us safe from harm.

Guiding Lights

Whenever my sailor husband was assigned to sea duty, I would stay with my mother in Brownwood, Texas. During one such visit in 1954, we drove to a family reunion with my two daughters, Faye, three years old, and Sissie, almost two. When the reunion ended, the weather looked stormy, but my mother and I decided to head home anyway.

The highway took us through small towns and rural areas of Texas. Momma wanted to stop at Wiley, the all-black college where I received my degree in biology in 1947. To pay for my schooling, Momma had worked as a pastry chef, and Wiley was a monument of sorts to the years she spent baking hundreds of pies, cakes, and cookies.

But we had a ten-hour drive ahead of us, and dark clouds were gathering. The temperature was falling, so we stopped to put sweaters on the girls, and Momma sat in the backseat between them. Opening the box of sandwiches we had brought along, she passed one to me and said, "Don't worry about us. We're as warm as toast."

But I was worried. It was hard for me to see. If I had known then that I had night blindness, I would have tried to find a place to stop. But being black meant that we could not just pull into a motel and wait out the storm. Segregation still prevailed.

When night came, the falling snow curtained off the sky. Not even the moon and stars were visible. When I pulled into a truck stop to get gas, I told the station attendant that I could scarcely see the road. He was really concerned when he realized I intended to keep driving.

Foolishly, I got back into the car with my mother and my two babies and started out again. I soon realized I could not see the road. It was as though we were in a dark cave, and I began to panic. I couldn't see to go forward; I couldn't see to turn around. Pulling off to the side of the road was out of the question, as I could not see that either. I wasn't even sure that I was on the road!

I tried to pray, but I was almost paralyzed with fear.
Briefly, I put my head on the steering wheel and
rubbed my eyes in hopes of seeing better. When I
looked up, I saw lights approaching in the rearview
mirror. The lights turned out to be from two 18-
wheelers. One drove around in front of my car and
slowed down. The other stayed behind us, its lights
casting a welcome glow inside the car. I knew in my
heart that the man at the gas station had told those
truckers about my predicament, and they had decided
to help. God had answered the prayer I could not utter.

I nestled between the hovering vehicles like a chick
taking refuge under its mother's wings. We traveled for
some time this way, and then I saw the right-turn
signal light blinking on the leading truck. The driver
flashed his headlights several times as a way of saying
good-bye before he turned onto another road. For a
moment I was terrified to be back in the darkness, but
then the truck that had been behind me pulled out in
front and continued to act as my guide.

It was dawn when we finally got back to Brownwood.
I blew my horn and waved at the trucker. He lowered
his window and smiled as he waved back. I never

knew the names of those drivers who helped deliver us safely home, but I will be forever grateful for the help they gave us on that stormy night.

Dear Father, when I am in danger, you never leave me alone. Whenever I am afraid, I call on you, and you're there, taking my hand and leading me to safety. You are the one who always walks with me, and I praise you for protecting my life. In Jesus' name. Amen.

The name of the Lord is a strong tower; the righteous run into it and are safe.

Proverbs 18:10

Lord God, whenever I have a "close call," I'm reminded of your protective presence in my life. I'm certain that I have many more brushes with danger than I am aware of, but you

*faithfully keep me from harm, even when I don't know it.
Thank you for reminding me that I am not walking alone;
please lead me into your good purposes for my life. Amen.*

[The Lord] *"led out his people like
sheep, and guided them in the
wilderness like a flock. He led them in
safety, so that they were not afraid."*

Psalm 78:52–53

The presence of danger produces one of two responses
in us: anxiety or faith. Often when we sense danger,
our first inclination is to become anxious. (Of course,
recoiling from danger is a good, God-given instinct,
but being terrorized by it is not our heavenly Father's
desire for us.) God wants his children to trust in him
no matter what circumstances may seem to threaten
their safety and security. Learning this kind of trust,
however, requires that danger come into our lives from

time to time. Our faith in God's protection then grows through these experiences, and we develop a wonderful peace of mind that cannot be shaken.

Gracious Father, I see how you are building my faith by allowing circumstances that challenge my sense of safety and security. I thank you that I am learning to trust in you. Today as I walk with you in the protection of your presence, grant that this peace of heart and mind I have right now will remain strong no matter what dangers may come my way.

David, the author of Psalm 23, said this when he faced danger: "I fear no evil; for you are with me." David did not say that bad things would never touch his life; he only said that such things were not to be feared because of God's presence.

It is the same for us. Our protection in life does not consist in avoiding all pain, difficulty, or even death. Our mortality is real, evil is real, pain is real, and in life, we will face each. But when we find our security in

God himself, none of these things can cause fear because we know that God will never leave us alone. And when life is done, he will carry us to the safety of our eternal home with him.

The Lord is faithful; he will strengthen you and guard you from the evil one.

2 Thessalonians 3:3

Lord, you keep my soul safe from harm. Though danger may threaten my very life, I have no cause to fear it. Your presence surrounds my life, and I am resting in your arms today. Thank you that I belong to you and that you will never leave me alone. I rejoice in the security of your protecting power!

An early morning explosion shattered windows all up and down the block. A house in the middle of the block had blown up and was reduced to splintered boards and rubble. The site looked like a war zone. And yet the woman who owned the house had emerged with only singed hair and ringing ears. Her dog had survived as well.

Reports of the accident revealed that a pilot light had gone out, and the woman had gone (with her dog) to the basement to light it again. Unfortunately, there had been a gas leak, and as soon as she struck the match, it was as if a bomb had been detonated. The woman should not have survived, but she did.

How often God shows his miraculous power in keeping us safe! From time to time, it can be a great exercise to review all of the times we can remember that God has kept us from harm. He truly watches over our lives!

Those of steadfast mind you keep in peace—in peace because they trust in you. Trust in the Lord forever, for in the Lord God you have an everlasting rock.

Isaiah 26:3–4

Driving from Indianapolis to Chicago one winter, I was caught in a blizzard. I had known it was coming, but I figured if I started out early enough, I could get home before it hit. I was mistaken. I was less than ten miles down the road when it hit, but two things— foolish optimism and concern that I would miss work the following day—motivated me to drive on. It was a bad decision.

Being from the West Coast, I was not fully aware of the peril. My windshield wipers kept freezing over, my headlights and taillights became blocked by snow, and I could not see even a few feet in front of me. For miles and miles I could only guess where the road was, and I didn't know if in the next moment I would smash into another car or one would smash into me. Any exit ramps I passed along the way were invisible in the whiteout conditions. But I drove on because I felt that stopping was more dangerous than continuing. And as I drove, I prayed feverishly.

Looking back, I am amazed that I made it safely home. I had been very foolish. God could have abandoned me to the consequences of my bad decision, but he did not. He stayed with me and helped me navigate that treacherous roadway all the way home.

The Lord bless you and keep you; the Lord make his face to shine upon you, and be gracious to you; the Lord lift up his countenance upon you, and give you peace.

Numbers 6:24–26

Because God loves us and is all powerful, we sometimes mistakenly think that trouble should never come our way. Sure, we can accept minor annoyances and challenges, but we think we should be exempt from the really big hardships. What is God for, anyway? God is good to us, not because he has shielded us from all harm, but because he comes to our aid when the blows do come.

Lord God, your power to protect me when danger is near keeps me from being anxious. Thank you for all the times and all the ways (the ones I am aware of as well as the ones I am not) that you have guarded my life through the years. Help me remember that no matter how the circumstances of my life may seem to threaten my safety and security, I can be confident that I will never walk alone in them because I am safe in your eternal presence. Amen.

CHAPTER 11

When We Doubt God's Goodness

*W*hen bad things happen to us for no apparent reason or when God seems remote and silent, a chill of doubt can creep in and settle over our faith. Are you angry with me, God? Have you forgotten me? These and other doubting questions fill our minds and eventually can spill over into our relationship with God. While we believe God exists, we may begin to wonder if he will remember to be good to us. What follows will remind readers that God walks with us through every test of faith, staying close beside us, even when we are tempted to doubt his goodness.

Just Friends

❖·———ॐ———·❖

I step into the elevator in the hospital where my wife
works and reach to push the button for the tenth
floor. Someone yells for me to hold the elevator. I
keep the doors open, and a young man steps inside.

"What floor?" I ask.

"Ten," he says.

I push the button, and the elevator starts going up. I try
not to stare at the young man but find it difficult. He
appears to be in his teens, but he's very thin and
completely bald. An IV in his left hand is connected
to a bag filled with fluid. The bag hangs on an IV pole
with wheels on the bottom. The young man glares
straight ahead at the elevator doors, and I continue to
sneak glances at him. I want to start a conversation, but
I doubt he'd be open to speaking with me, so we ride
silently to the tenth floor.

The elevator stops, and the doors open. The young man makes his way off the elevator as I hold the doors open. I notice that his IV is leaking fluid.

"Excuse me," I say. "Your IV is leaking."

"So what," the man snaps. "I'm going to die anyway."

He exits the elevator, and I stand there in shock. After a few moments, I walk down the hall to the nurse's station where my wife is working.

"What's wrong, honey?" she asks. "You look upset."

"I was just on the elevator with a teenage boy, and I told him his IV was leaking. He said it didn't matter because he was going to die anyway. He looked so depressed—I just feel really bad for him."

"Oh, that must be Nathan. He has leukemia and needs a bone marrow transplant, but they're having a hard time finding a donor."

"What about his family?"

"He doesn't know his father or have any immediate relatives, and his mother isn't a match. They're searching all across the country, but it's not looking very good."

"Can I talk to him?"

"You can try. He's not very receptive right now."

"I feel like I need to speak to him."

"Okay. He's down the hall in room 1013. Good luck."

I walk down the hall to Nathan's room and knock on the door. No one answers, so I step inside. The room is silent and dark. I can faintly see Nathan seated in the corner of the room.

"What do you want?" Nathan snaps.

"I was in the elevator with you a few minutes ago," I say.

"So what?"

I could see this wouldn't be easy. "I just wanted to come by and talk to you."

Silence.

"Is there anything I can do for you?" I ask.

"Yeah," Nathan says, "you can leave."

His harsh words ring in my ears. Even though I feel bad for him, it's clear he doesn't want to talk to me. I lower my head and slowly turn to leave the room. But in spite of my initial disappointment, I feel compelled to give it another try.

I turn back around and look at him. "Nathan," I say, "I was just hoping that we could be friends."

"What?" he asks, surprised.

"I said I was hoping we could be friends."

I slowly take a few steps toward Nathan and notice that he is crying. I open the curtain to let in some light and see that Nathan is holding a small book against his chest.

"What have you got there?" I ask.

"It's where I write down all my prayers. Every time I ask God for something I write it in this book."

"The book looks pretty thick. You must have a lot of prayers in there."

"Yeah. I was going to throw it away before you walked into the room."

"Why were you going to do that?"

"I was getting frustrated with God because he hasn't answered any of my prayers."

I'm not quite sure what to say next. It's easy to understand Nathan's frustration. I watch as he opens his book. He quietly flips through it, then stops on a page near the end. He stares at it intently.

"Are you still going to throw the book away?" I ask.

"No," Nathan says.

"What changed your mind?"

Nathan holds the book out toward me, and I walk over and take it. I glance down at the page and begin to read. The letter has yesterday's date at the top.

"Dear God,

I know I ask you for a lot of things. I'm not sure you're listening because it seems like none of my prayers have been answered. You know my situation and what I need, so I won't ask again. There is only one thing that I want right now. If you answer this prayer then I'll know you truly care about me. The only thing I really want is a friend. Love, Nathan"

I look up at Nathan with tears in my eyes, marveling that God would use me as the answer to someone's prayer. "I'm glad we're going to be friends," I tell him. "Me, too," Nathan says. "Me, too."

Lord God, when I call out to you and it seems as though you are silent, I struggle to believe that you care about me. Please help me when my faith is weak; don't let my doubts get the best of me. Thank you for continuing to walk with me, even when I struggle with doubt.

Jesus said, "All things can be done for the one who believes." Immediately the father of the child cried out, "I believe; help my unbelief!"

Mark 9:23-24

Father, when it seems you have forgotten to be good to me, remind me to look at the blessings in my life—all the ways you have shown your goodness to me already—so that I won't lose heart. Let my doubts become swallowed up in faith today as I trust in your promises. In Jesus' name. Amen.

Now faith is the assurance of things hoped for, the conviction of things not seen. . . . And without faith it is impossible to please God, for whoever

would approach him must believe that he exists and that he rewards those who seek him.

Hebrews 11:1, 6

When she didn't have to work at Boeing, Tanya would come to our Saturday morning coffee group. From time to time I would ask her how things were going, and each time she opened up her heart to me, her faith always amazed me. One point in time stands out in particular: Tanya needed major surgery, her younger brother had just died in a car accident, her supervisor was demanding and unreasonable, and her ex-husband (who had walked out on her and their son a couple of years earlier) was harassing her regularly.

Tanya didn't hold back the tears when her circumstances seemed overwhelming, but she never expressed doubt in God's goodness. "I don't know what his purposes are in all of this," she would say, "but I know that he works all things together for good to those who love him, and I love him with all my heart."

If she ever doubted God, she simply chose to believe his promises rather than to trust her own thoughts. As a result, she has maintained a close walk with God, one that keeps getting better and better, no matter what comes to challenge her faith in him.

Dear Jesus, Scripture says you were tempted in the same ways I am tempted. So you must know how this trial tempts me to doubt your goodness. I want to believe you are near me, but I don't feel your nearness, and you don't seem to hear me. It's getting harder and harder to have faith, so please show me how to believe that you are right here walking beside me and that you will see me through this struggle.

God wants to give us good things, but not just any good things. He desires the best things for his children, and these *best* things are often of an eternal nature. For example, we might ask for finances, but God knows that we have a deeper need for faith, so he may permit a financial setback to hit us to spur us to grow in our faith. He will always provide for our basic needs, but his desire to bless us reaches not only into time but also clear into eternity.

So when you are tempted to doubt God's goodness because of adversity, take some time to ponder the possibility that he may be in the process of giving you some blessing of surpassing eternal worth, something you've always wanted but didn't think possible. God is good, and his best blessings are forever.

If any of you is lacking in wisdom, ask God, who gives to all generously and ungrudgingly, and it will be given you. But ask in faith, never doubting, for the one who doubts is like a wave of the sea, driven and tossed by the wind.

James 1:5–6

Father, I'm struggling with doubt as I ask you for things that I've asked for before. Help me pray with faith and not be discouraged by the fact that I have not seen an answer yet to my prayers. I know you are teaching me to trust your timing and wisdom. So I'll take your hand in faith as I walk and talk with you today. Amen.

Someone is called a "doubting Thomas" when they won't believe something unless they see it with their own eyes. The label is a reference to one of Jesus' disciples. After Jesus' resurrection, he appeared to a number of his disciples, but Thomas wasn't among these first ones to see the risen Christ. When Thomas's fellow disciples assured him that Jesus was alive, Thomas would not believe it. "Unless I see for myself," the doubting disciple said, "I won't believe you."

When we are going through a trial and our faith is tested, we can rise above Thomas-type thinking by allowing ourselves to receive encouragement from fellow believers. Others who have been where we are and who have experienced God's faithfulness are gifts from God; they can help us leave our doubts behind.

Then Jesus said to Thomas, "Put your finger here and see my hands. Reach out your hand and put it in my side. Do not doubt but believe." Then Jesus said to him, "Have you believed because you have seen me? Blessed are those who have not seen and yet have come to believe."

John 20:27, 29

Doubt is a crossroads that we come to many times in life. When we doubt God's goodness, one direction open to us is the way of faith, the other is the way of unbelief. As we stand at that juncture, which way will we choose? The way of faith has the promises of God to stand on as well as the testimony of many who have experienced his goodness. The way of unbelief has disappointment, despair, bitterness, addiction—a downward spiral of hopelessness. The life of faith does not guarantee a bed of roses, but it does guarantee a relationship with God that will not fail and an eternal home with him when this life draws to a close.

I will say to the Lord, "My refuge and my fortress; my God, in whom I trust."

Psalm 91:2

Lord Jesus, I don't see the light at the end of this tunnel of circumstance. But I don't need to see the outcome to keep doubt away; I just need to be certain that you will walk with me all the way through it. Your word promises that I will never walk alone because you always walk with me. So I stand, in faith, on that promise today. In your name. Amen.

CHAPTER 12

He Frees Us from Depression

*A*nyone whose spirit has ever been taken over by depression knows what it feels like to have the desire for life grow weaker and weaker. Disappointment, fear, hopelessness, helplessness, anxiety . . . these debilitating emotions can overwhelm us and send us into a deep depression. Then, as we try to escape and hide from life and others, isolation becomes our prison, and we feel absolutely alone. Even in our depression, however, God does not leave us alone. He is ready to set us free; we need only call out to him and then take his hand as he leads us to freedom.

A Special Shopping Trip

•◆•————◦⟨ᴗ⟩◦————•◆•

It was just after Christmas, and the supply of groceries in our house had dwindled to little more than starches. I knew I had to go to the grocery store, but it was something I always dreaded. Since my husband had moved out (to make a "fresh start" with a high school girlfriend), my finances had barely been enough to provide for me and my children. Whenever we went shopping, the kids asked for things I couldn't afford, and I hated having to deny them every single time.

I got my two-year-old twins and my seven- and nine-year-olds ready to go, and we all headed for the store. By the time we finally made it to the checkout line, the twins were fussy and hungry, and I was exhausted. I had been praying for patience and a financial blessing that week, and I wasn't feeling confident about either one at the moment. It seemed as though, even when I tried to cut corners, something unexpected always came up and wiped out what little money I had managed to save.

When it was my turn at the register, I pulled out my debit card to pay for my $78 grocery bill. I was incredulous when the cashier gave me a little piece of paper stating that the card issuer had denied the charge. "That's impossible," I said. "I just made a deposit this morning!"

I grew increasingly embarrassed as I saw the line grow behind me. A pretty, young woman directly behind me was neatly lining up her groceries. I thought momentarily of how tidy and organized she seemed, and I felt a pang of jealousy at her composure and style. I was suddenly very self-conscious of my shabby coat and frumpy look.

"I can run your card through again, if you'd like," the cashier offered kindly.

"Sure. Okay," I mumbled.

"Sorry," she said again after a moment. She told me she could subtotal the groceries for me to take care of later, and I was relieved that I would no longer be holding up the long line. I took the kids and stepped away from the cash register as the cashier finished subtotaling my items, and baggers put all my groceries into bags to be set aside.

The children were growing more restless, and I was disappointed that we'd have to leave empty-handed and come back later to pick up our food. The weight of despair began to settle on my shoulders. I'd been trying to maintain a positive attitude around the children, especially because I knew it was hard on them when their father left. But it was getting more difficult all the time for me not to break down in front of the kids. Standing in that grocery store, I felt sad and anxious and alone. God seemed very far away indeed, and I felt forsaken.

I'd been busy tending to the children and trying to stay out of the way of other shoppers, but I happened to look up and notice the young woman who'd been in line behind me just as she walked out of the store with her groceries. At that moment, the cashier called me back to the register. I figured she was probably done tallying up the subtotal for my groceries.

"The lady who was behind you in line paid for your groceries," the cashier told me, smiling. "So you can take them all with you now."

I was shocked. "What? Are you sure? You're kidding!"

"No," the cashier said, beaming. "Happy New Year!"

After I loaded the kids and groceries into the car, I started to cry. What an unexpected blessing I'd just received! A woman I had never met before had just made a huge impact on my life. My feelings of despair and loneliness disappeared, and I was sorry that I'd ever felt forsaken by God. He had sent an angel into my life who not only paid for my material needs but who also gave me a boost in spirit that was absolutely priceless.

Jesus, you know how overwhelmed I feel by the things I cannot control or fix or change. Depression seems to be my normal state of existence. I can hardly remember what it feels like to have joy in my heart. Please come help me! I need to know that you are still with me and that you have the power to free me.

*Why are you cast down, O my soul,
and why are you disquieted within me?
Hope in God; for I shall again praise
him; my help and my God.*

Psalm 42:11

*Heavenly Father, fill my mind with truth today and help me
focus on it. The truth is that you love me; you are with me;
and nothing is too difficult for you. Lift my depressed spirit
today and remind me that you have good plans and purposes
in store for my life. Thank you for reminding me that as I
walk with you, I have a hope and a future. Amen.*

We are afflicted in every way, but not crushed; perplexed, but not driven to despair; persecuted, but not forsaken; struck down, but not destroyed.

2 Corinthians 4:8–9

Friends, counselors, therapists, or pastors may help us overcome depression, but only God knows precisely what the source is. He made us and understands us thoroughly. He sees into places of our heart and mind that no one else can. Certainly he may (and probably will) lead us to others who will help us, but even as we seek outside help, we can ask God to be the one guiding us to emotional healing and freedom. In fact, God longs for us to invite him in; for his desire for us is that we never walk alone, not through depression, nor any other struggle.

Lord Jesus, I know that you want to set me free from my depression and that you will do it. I need your help, though, to guide me to the right people and places where I will find your wisdom and counsel for my life. I'm thankful that you have already made a way for me and that now you are taking my hand to lead me in it. What a comfort to realize that I do not need to walk alone in this!

Comfort, O comfort my people, says your God. Speak tenderly to [them].

Isaiah 40:1–2

I look to you, Lord God, for encouragement today. Comfort me with your word, with people who will speak truth and love into my life, and with music that directs my thoughts to you. Keep me on this path of freedom from depression as I walk closely with you.

The depressing weight of your burden is crushing you, and God is inviting you to lay it down. But you hesitate. The burden is yours, after all. Who, but you, could possibly have the proper level of concern for it? Who could understand the immense weight of it and give it the respect it deserves? Who could shed the necessary tears over it, and who would lay awake at night to keep watch over it? Then you hear God gently remind you, "My child, I have already done all this and more. Jesus carried it all the way to the cross. Won't you lay it down now, dear child?"

So we do not lose heart. Even though our outer nature is wasting away, our inner nature is being renewed day by day. For this slight momentary affliction is preparing us for an eternal weight of glory beyond all measure.

2 Corinthians 4:16–17

When depression has a grip on us, it whispers a nasty lie: Life will always be this way; there is only this darkness and nothing else to look forward to. But let the truth be known: There are people—many, many people who have heard the same lie—who can testify that it is, indeed, a lie. They can tell you that there is a very real place of relief beyond the world of sadness and isolation. It's a place where light doesn't hurt your eyes anymore; instead, the light brings joy. It's a place where you remember to delight in springtime—and in all the seasons for that matter. The happiness you thought would never visit you again does return. And you have the strength and wisdom to lead others there as well, others who are suffering as you once did.

The way to this place isn't clear when you are still in darkness, but Jesus is the light of the world, and he knows the way. He wants to lead you there and will be with you every step of the way.

The spirit of the Lord God is upon me, because the Lord has anointed me; he has sent me to bring good news to the oppressed.... to give them a garland instead of ashes, the oil of gladness instead of mourning, the mantle of praise instead of a faint spirit.

Isaiah 61:1, 3

Lord Jesus, I call to you from this dark place in my soul, knowing that you are the light of the world. Please show me the way out of this prison of depression! I am ready to leave and follow you to where I can experience the wonder of life again. Thank you for not leaving me here alone; you are the one who has stayed with me and who will lead me along paths of joy and praise. Amen.

CHAPTER 13

A Healer for the Hurting

*A*s we go through life, we cannot avoid the sorrow of loss. Because those we love may leave us, our hearts hurt deeply, and healing can be difficult to find. But there is healing for those who seek it. The Scriptures tell us that Jesus was wounded for us so we could find restoration and healing in him. And though it is a spiritual mystery, we can experience healing that comes through his sacrifice. What a relief that we don't have to just cope with our hurting hearts! We have one who walks beside us, who leads us in the path of healing.

Front-Porch Petunias

Mid-September, I return to my chair on the front porch, holding on to the tail end of summer as it races away. The petunias in the wooden barrel beside me are beginning to fade. Their color is less vibrant now—sapped by the afternoon sun day after day. All summer long I have carefully pinched off the old flowers and been rewarded with bursts of new color. Each time I open my front door they greet me like an old familiar friend coming to visit.

On breezy days I have watched the petunias sway back and forth in a rolling motion like ocean waves. Even when it seems there is no breeze, the flowers have gently wobbled in the air, as if from angel's breath or the touch of God.

This is the time of year when I usually take out the petunias and plant flowers that will thrive during the autumn and winter. Last year on September 30, I wrote in my diary: "Ah, gorgeous, golden autumn." I pulled out the tired petunias and planted sprightly, springy pansies and snapdragons. The ground seemed to open up eagerly under my hands. It was as if the dirt itself was hungry for this new flower, just as we were for cool, refreshing autumn after the long, hot summer.

But this year, I am waiting a while. I am in no hurry. I am trying to hold on to the last traces of this summer. For it held much: It was a summer of change. In June, our son graduated from high school. In July, our 14-year-old dog was diagnosed with cancer. In August, our son joined the Navy and left home. In September, our dog died. And now my husband and I are trying to adjust to our empty nest. A lifetime of growing-up years, of childhood hustle and bustle, has suddenly turned quiet. Our dog, a silver-grey keeshond, is no longer found at his favorite place in the house, the corner near the front door where he'd curl up to sleep.

Through all these summer changes, the petunias on the front porch have been a steady source of comfort. Continually present, they have quietly renewed themselves, day after day. While human loss and change have stormed around me all summer long, the petunias have sent a silent reminder of nature's power to grow, to live, and to thrive, even in the midst of loss. They remind me to find strength in what remains behind... and of our never-ending capacity for fresh starts.

Our son is well, graduating soon from Navy basic training. He has a new life. My husband and I are strengthened by his spirit and enthusiasm. And although he is no longer here in our home, we send him our love and support in our letters and in our daily prayers. And memories of our dear old dog are here with us, too. In our hearts, he still walks with us. He still guards the front door, stationed at his favorite corner. By now, many of our friends have returned from vacations that took them to places as far away as Hawaii, Canada, and Paris. They have been renewed and invigorated by their travels. This summer my husband and I stayed home. We cared for our dog. We assisted our son with his transition from high school and home life to the military.

All during the long, hot, tumultuous months, these petunias have helped bring me to a state of peacefulness. They have refreshed my soul. I've realized that sometimes God makes his presence known to us in simple, unexpected ways. He gives us the grace to notice and feel the blessings of comfort in what is close to us. And sometimes those blessings can be found on our own front porch.

Jesus, thank you for all the ways you reach out to heal me with your gentle touch. When sorrow overwhelms me, you come with the balm of your presence to gently speak to my hurting heart. Make me able to receive the healing you bring as you remain with me today.

"I will restore health to you, and your wounds I will heal," says the Lord.

Jeremiah 30:17

Dear Father, restorer of grieving hearts, will you come and bring joy to my sad heart? Please help me bring today's hurts to you so they don't become bitter roots in my life. And show me how to heal from this pain so it doesn't continue to bring me down. Thank you for walking with me through this healing process. In Jesus' name. Amen.

I am lowly and in pain; let your salvation, O God, protect me.... Let the oppressed see it and be glad; you who seek God, let your hearts revive.

Psalm 69:29, 32

The wounds of the past can reach into our present, affecting our relationships and behavior in adverse ways. Anger, depression, and shame are just a few of the symptoms that point to such unhealed wounds. Until we effectively deal with those wounds they will continue to hinder us from enjoying the present. God knows the pathway that will lead to our freedom from these old hurts. He knows how to orchestrate the healing process. And when we are ready to begin, we need only ask him, and he will gently begin to lead us through it, walking with us from beginning to end.

Lord Jesus, it's hard for me to believe right now that I could ever recover from my loss. But I know you are a great healer. So here is my pain, and here are the reasons for it. Here are my tears, and here is my brokenness. I know you are gentle, so help me not push you away as you reach out to heal me. In your name. Amen.

When our love for others causes us to suffer, our instinct is to build walls around our heart to protect ourselves from being hurt again. The only problem with walling ourselves in is that, in doing so, we also wall out love. Jesus gave us an example that can help us keep our hearts open. After he learned that his cousin John the Baptist had been murdered, he withdrew to a quiet place to receive loving comfort from his heavenly Father. Jesus then turned outward to love others. When we take our wounds to our heavenly Father and allow him to comfort and heal us, we will find that we, too, can remain open to give and receive love.

Praise the Lord! . . . He heals the brokenhearted, and binds up their wounds.

Psalm 147:1, 3

Father, you come quickly to heal me when I call on you. You may heal me in a single moment or you may choose to work through a process over time, but either way you restore my soul with your wisdom and power. I give you praise today for what you are doing in my life as you walk with me, step by step, to wholeness.

God wants to heal our hearts. For from our hearts, the Scriptures say, flow the issues of life. Real life is lived from the inside, and we cannot fully live—even with whole bodies—if our hearts are not made whole in Christ. Indeed, many people with physical conditions or challenges are living life to the fullest because their hearts have been made whole.

Take a moment to consider these words: God *longs* to heal your heart. He wants to lead you into a life as he intended it to be lived—with joy from the inside out.

But you, O Lord my Lord, act on my behalf for your name's sake; because your steadfast love is good, deliver me. For I am poor and needy, and my heart is pierced within me....Help me, O Lord my God! Save me according to your steadfast love.

Psalm 109:21–22, 26

In the physical realm, some wounds require surgery while others call for just ointment and a bandage. In the realm of the heart, our wounds also cover a wide range of severity with their corresponding diversity of treatments. Fortunately, God is a specialist at healing our hearts, for he is able to see into each one. We can trust, therefore, that he has the right skill and perfect wisdom to tend to each of our wounds. And his gentle presence remains with us through the entire procedure . . . and beyond.

Surely he has borne our infirmities and carried our diseases; . . . upon him was the punishment that made us whole, and by his bruises we are healed.

Isaiah 53:4–5

Lord Jesus, you came to heal my hurting heart. I want to experience your healing power, so please help me trust your gentleness and your wisdom as you reach in to touch the wounded places in my soul. Some of this healing needs to reach back into my past; some of it I need for more recent wounds. But all of it comes from you, so I look to you as my source, and I cling to you, thanking you for being with me as I walk this new path of healing. In your name. Amen.

CHAPTER 14

With Us in the Shadow of Death

*T*he shepherd-psalmist David wrote: "Though I walk through the valley of the shadow of death, I will fear no evil, for you are with me." There is perhaps no other time when we desire more intensely to know God is with us than when death draws near, and if it were not for the One who walked with us, we would feel very much alone. But God is there. Our Lord is the gentlest of guides, who can help us through each valley. And because he is with us, we need never walk alone.

A Gift of Time

Feeling unusually weak, sick to my stomach, and unable to eat, I decided it was time to pay a visit to the doctor. His written instructions included a three-day water diet followed by a medication that would clear my system for an X-ray.

When it was time to take the medicine, though, I had the strongest impression that I should not take it. It was a familiar impression—one I'd learned to pay attention to over the years. In fact, I was certain the Lord was telling me "Whoa!" that I wrote the word *whoa* on the doctor's instruction sheet! (A friend and I laughed later at my confident inscription.) But that morning when a call came, telling me the X-ray machine was broken and I shouldn't go through with the medication, I wasn't exactly surprised.

As it turned out, further examination of my condition revealed that the little *whoa* spoken gently but firmly by the Savior literally saved my life. Had I taken the prescribed treatment, I would have died painfully and alone in a matter of minutes.

I've been diagnosed with an inoperable tumor just beyond the outlet of my stomach. Soon I will be with the Lord, . . . but not *too* soon. God's *whoa* has given me time to say last things to those I hold dear. And while I'm grateful to be surrounded by their caring ways and prayers, I'm grateful, most of all, to be assured of the presence of the One whose love and mercy surround us all from life's beginning to its end.

Gentle Lord Jesus, you hold my heart with such tenderness and compassion. Thank you that you never scold me for my tears nor turn away when I cannot pray. Instead, you weep with me, wait with me, and give me quiet tokens of your understanding. I can feel you healing my heart with your careful love. I'm so glad you are here with me. Amen.

The promise of resurrection is repeated to us each year in the metaphor of spring. New life bounds forth out of the cold, lifeless winter, and in that awakening God whispers hope to our hearts, reminding us to believe in his power to raise us up again to eternal life. Each time the first crocuses push through the soil, each time the birds return from migration, each time the barren trees are clothed again (as if overnight) in green, God announces that death is not the final word in the life of his children. We will live again—and forever—with him in paradise.

For I am convinced that neither death, nor life, . . . nor anything else in all creation, will be able to separate us from the love of God in Christ Jesus our Lord.

Romans 8:38–39

Heavenly Father, you offered up your Son's life so that I could have hope even when facing death. Please keep that hope before me so I do not despair today. Remind me that I will be reunited one day with loved ones who love you. Amen.

For to me, living is Christ and dying is gain.

Philippians 1:21

Our moments and days and years are in God's hands, and he will not lose one of them. As we entrust ourselves completely to him, more and more we lose the fear of the future, and especially the fear of death. Death may still wound our hearts, but it can never destroy our faith or banish our hope. For we know beyond a doubt that God's great love has found us, has granted us an eternal home, and will never leave us to walk alone through any part of our journey. To the end of our days, our God walks with us.

Heavenly Father, I belong to you. You made me, gave me life, and have granted me a journey on this earth. Prepare my heart and mind for the day you will take me to live in my true home with you. I delight in the life you have granted me here, and I know I will delight even more in the life you have prepared for me in your presence. Walk closely with me now, I pray, as I continue on my journey toward home.

If we live, we live to the Lord, and if we die, we die to the Lord; so then, whether we live or whether we die, we are the Lord's.

Romans 14:8

Lord, I trust in your resurrection power over death, but I struggle with the thought of being parted from the people I love. I know you understand; death separated you from your Son for a time. So please stay close to me. Grant me strength of heart and peace of mind. In Jesus' name. Amen.

For more than six years, I watched my grandfather suffer through cancer. I had grown to love him even more than when I was a child, for now (in his illness) he had set aside his stoicism and had opened his heart to me. I spent a good deal of time visiting with him toward the very end of his struggle. As I said my final good-bye to him just before I made the long cross-country trip back to college, we both cried. It was the last time we were together. His love is still with me, though. It is strong and sweet, and it speaks to me across time and eternity. I know it waits for me, and so I press on with purpose, believing life is worth living, if for no other reason, for the wonder of loving and being loved.

Jesus said to Martha, "I am the resurrection and the life. Those who believe in me, even though they die, will live, and everyone who lives and believes in me will never die."

John 11:25–26

Dear loving Father, you have been very good to me during the years you've walked with me. I feel your presence even more than when we first walked together. And now, as I see my days here on earth becoming fewer, I rejoice that I will see you far clearer than I ever have when I enter into your heavenly kingdom.

Fill my heart with your peace and your joy, knowing that you will never leave me and that you have arranged a special home for me in heaven, where I will rejoin my beloved friends and family. Thank you for keeping me safe from fears and doubt during the closing years of my life. Amen.

The good things of earth are just a shadow of the wonders of heaven. The Scriptures tell us that no eye has seen nor ear heard nor heart begun to conceive of how God has prepared our eternal home to delight us. The old notion that we will be in some state of mindless bliss as we float aimlessly on clouds and strum endlessly on harps is badly off the mark. The God who created the majesty of the mountains, the awesomeness of the oceans, the variety of wildlife, the glory of sunrise, and the mystery of the night sky promises something even more spectacular on the other side of this life on earth. So we can walk with him today in full confidence, for we have a glorious future, and he will be with us now and forever.

Jesus said, "Do not let your hearts be troubled. Believe in God; believe also in me. In my Father's house there are

many dwelling places. If it were not so, would I have told you that I go to prepare a place for you? And if I go and prepare a place for you, I will come again and take you to myself, so that where I am, there you may be also."

John 14:1–3

Jesus, I am walking through the valley of the shadow of death. Let me sense your presence. Speak comfort to my heart by your Spirit and through your word. Help me press on, knowing that a day of joyful reunion lies ahead. Thank you that even though I am walking through this dark valley, I am not alone. You are always with me. In your name I pray these things. Amen.

CHAPTER 15

He Loves the Unloved

*O*ur *greatest emotional need is to feel loved, and God's desire is that our human relationships be characterized by his love. Unfortunately life doesn't always happen that way. God's love is good news, however, especially to the unloved, for he has a special place in his heart for those who have been left alone on the outside of human love. When we feel unloved, he reaches into our lives with parental affection and compassion, assuring us with his own loving presence that we need never walk alone in this world.*

My Father's Love

They say you can't miss what you never had, but I say they're wrong. My parents divorced when I was just one, and growing up without a dad definitely left a painful void in my life. Even though I'd never known his face or the warmth of his hand taking mine, I still missed his presence.

When I was 13, some friends and I met at a church parking lot to shoot hoops. It turned out to be my first attempt to find the love I craved.

"Josh, don't go home, man," Michael urged, wiping sweat from his forehead after we finished our game. "Come to church with us. It starts in a few minutes."

At first I intended to say no, but something drew me. It wasn't a hunger for God or the hope I would find something life-changing between those concrete walls, but more of a need to be included in whatever my friends were doing. It felt good to simply belong.

The preacher addressed the congregation with words that flowed in a powerful stream, but I yawned and shifted uncomfortably. At the end of the evening I bowed my head, but only because that's what everyone else was doing and I didn't want to be different. I was tired of being different and feeling alone.

The more I tried to find what was missing inside of me, the more lost I became. Marijuana could mask the pain for a while, filling me with a hazy sense of relief until the high vanished and I had to face reality again. Alcohol dulled my suffering and gave me a shield to hide behind until a hangover was all that was left. Still, a temporary escape was better than none at all, and I clung to that reasoning like those church people clung to their Bibles.

Smoking and drinking were nothing I would do in front of friends or family, only in the privacy of my room. I was still "good old Josh" to everyone who knew me, pulling in straight A's, hanging out with friends, and functioning like a well-oiled machine, but there was that other side of me that only I knew, the one that surfaced in the dark. I tried so hard to fill the void in my life that I found poor substitutes in booze and weed. At least they were always there when I needed them . . . joints and whiskey bottles never walked away.

That summer I met a girl named Stephanie through a mutual friend. She was bright, pretty, and easy to talk with. We began dating, and the closer I got to her, the less my needy soul hurt. She and her parents were devout Christians, which meant I had to do some heavy acting. If Stephanie was going to love me and chase all my troubles away, I would have to play the role of a Christian. I knew I could do it; it hadn't been that hard the night I went to church with Michael and Brian. I just needed to go through the motions of worship again.

Countless Sundays passed as I attended church to be with Stephanie. Her parents nodded approvingly as we all sang from the hymn books and whispered together in prayer. I became the world's greatest pretender. Who would ever guess that just the night before I had fallen asleep in a cloud of marijuana smoke with an empty bottle in my hand? It was a juggling act that was becoming second nature to me.

One afternoon, Stephanie announced that she was going on a retreat with girls from church and would be out of town for three days. I didn't realize until that weekend just how vital Stephanie was to me. She was the most important thing in my world, and I was facing a whole weekend without her.

"There's a party at Steve's place," my friend Scott said one Friday night. "It'd be cool if you could be there."

His invitation sounded great until I remembered Stephanie's parents. There was an important revival at the church that night, and they were expecting me to be there.

"Can't," I answered remorsefully. "I've got other plans."

The church was filling quickly as I searched for Stephanie's parents. A slight pounding in my skull was the only trace of how wasted I'd gotten the night before. I was missing Stephanie so much. I felt empty without her. All the more reason to straighten the knotted silk tie at my throat and sit with her parents, except I arrived late and their pew was filled. They smiled and waved as I sat in the third row.

The pastor explained that they had a special guest that evening. A 17-year-old boy would deliver a personal testimony of what God had done in his life. I watched as the kid shook hands with the pastor and then took command of the microphone. He wore jeans, a T-shirt, and sneakers. His blond hair hung long and shaggy to his shoulders.

"My father loves me," he opened by stating. "It took me 17 years to be able to say those words. My father loves me, and he will love me no matter what mistakes I make or what weaknesses I have. He will love me through every storm in my life and hold me in his embrace until the clouds clear and the sun streams through again."

The wounds I carried from my own uncaring father began to sting as if scoured with salt. This kid had a great dad who obviously loved him very much. I stared at him with envy.

"I'm not speaking of my mortal father," the young man said, scanning the congregation with pale blue eyes. "My mortal father was incapable of love. He abused me throughout my childhood and beat my mom until she could barely stand. What meant the most to him was his vodka, which eventually took his life."

My mouth grew dry. The people seated around me began to melt away, and all I could see was this boy, virtually the same age I was, drawing me into a world I knew too well—a world with a big puzzle piece missing.

"When I say my father loves me, I'm speaking of my real father... your real father... the father that will embrace you for all of eternity." He paused, pinning his gaze on me. "I'm talking about my spiritual father."

I listened to every word he said. He spoke of God as our true father, the one who will never abandon us, turn away from us, or disappoint us. He said that knowing God and letting him into your life will bring you the most awesome parent/child relationship you could ever experience.

By the time he closed with a heartfelt prayer, I was sobbing as I bowed my head. For once, my prayer came from my heart.

I could hardly wait to talk to Stephanie when she got back from the retreat. I would no longer have to pretend. Now my love for God was as real as hers.

"I've got news for you," she said.

I grinned. "I've got news, too. Me first, okay? If I don't tell you this minute, I'm going to explode!"

I explained about the revival and how God spoke to me that night and how he told me that he is my loving father and I don't need to hurt anymore. I told her that my life had been forever changed, and it was all because of the Lord.

Stephanie hugged me before her expression clouded. "We need to break up," she said softly. "I do love you. It's nothing you did—I just feel the need to concentrate on my relationship with God right now. I hope you understand."

As I walked home with her words in my mind, all that had happened recently began to make sense. God had saved me and finally shown me where I belonged. The love and acceptance I had always searched for wasn't in a booze bottle or a marijuana high. It wasn't even in my relationship with Stephanie. Those were all temporary hiding places so I wouldn't have to face my pain. My real place of love and belonging was in the arms of my heavenly Father. I knew I'd never feel abandoned again.

At the time of this writing, I am attending Bible college. God is calling me to preach to inner-city teens, which I plan to do upon graduation. My dream is to one day stand in a pulpit, looking out into the eyes of lost young people, and say the words that changed my life just three short years ago: "My name is Josh, and I want to tell everyone that my father truly loves me."

Heavenly Father, I crave love. Thank you for giving yours to me freely and completely. I have felt unloved by others at times, but I have learned that your love is steady and strong. I can rest in it, knowing it will be there tomorrow... and for all my tomorrows.

See what love the Father has given us, that we should be called children of God; and that is what we are.

1 John 3:1

God's love is not a consolation prize; it is the *grand* prize. If we push past God's love in an attempt to grab hold of human imitations of it, we'll miss out. Ignoring God's love might even be compared to trampling a winning lottery ticket as we rush to collect a monthly paycheck!

God is the *source* of all love. God is the *author* of loving relationships. And God *is* love. That is why the amazing gift of human love finds its true significance only in the context of God's love. And that is why when we feel unloved, a relationship with God is the best place to begin our quest for love.

Father, sometimes in my strong desire to experience love, I reach out to all kinds of people and things instead of drawing near to you. But only you know how to satisfy my need to feel loved, so help me stop grasping at straws. I'm so tired of trying to do this my way. Please lead me to your love that will stay with me always.

Love songs are a staple of music radio. Songs of love lost, love found, love in trouble, love on fire, and so on—they continually fill the airwaves in almost every style of music. There's no doubt that we love to sing and hear songs about love.

The Book of Psalms has many of its own love songs written to praise the greatest love of all: God's love. Think back to the last time you sang a song to express how you feel about God's love for you. Singing love songs to God encourages the unloved person's heart with the message of acceptance and fills their mind with the truth that God loves them ... forever.

He Loves the Unloved ❖

> *I will sing of your steadfast love, O Lord, forever; with my mouth I will proclaim your faithfulness to all generations. I declare that your steadfast love is established forever; your faithfulness is as firm as the heavens.*

Psalm 89:1–2

God, your love is good and faithful! Thank you for opening my eyes to see how much you love me. As I begin to walk in your acceptance and kindness, help me heal from past wounds of feeling unloved. Thank you that I won't be walking through this process alone because you walk with me.

To feel truly loved for the first time is a powerful experience. For many people, the first time they've felt love is when they encountered God as they began a new relationship with him. What a powerful experience to have God's love—the best of all loves—to be the first to fill your unloved heart!

Scripture is clear on this point: God wants a loving relationship with us. He is not angry, disappointed, or frustrated with us. He is not our earthly parents, our boss, or our spouse. He is the God who would sacrifice anything to give us his love, and his love is higher, longer, wider, deeper than any we could ever imagine. And it is for us.

For God so loved the world that he gave his only Son, so that everyone who believes in him may not perish but may have eternal life.

John 3:16

What's the shortest path to finding love? The message of John 3:16 (the verse on page 190) spells it out for us. God has shown his love to us in the Lord Jesus Christ. So when we embrace Jesus—God's love-gift—we find our embrace is returned in the greatest expression of love ever.

The Lord said, "I have loved you with an everlasting love; therefore I have continued my faithfulness to you."

Jeremiah 31:3

My loving Father, how sweet your kindness and compassion are toward me. I receive them with joy and gratitude. I also embrace your love as you have shown it to me in your Son, Jesus. I realize right now I am not unloved. I am deeply loved by you. That is why I know I will never walk alone. Amen.

Footprints in the Sand

One night I dreamed I was walking
Along the beach with the Lord.
Many scenes from my life flashed across the sky.
In each scene I noticed footprints in the sand.
This bothered me because I noticed that
During the low periods of my life when I was
Suffering from anguish, sorrow, or defeat,
I could see only one set of footprints,
So I said to the Lord, "You promised me,
Lord, that if I followed You,
You would walk with me always.
But I noticed that during the most trying periods
Of my life there have only been
One set of prints in the sand.
Why, when I have needed You most,
You have not been there for me?"
The Lord replied,
"The times when you have seen only one set of footprints
Is when I carried you."

—Mary Stevenson